Reptiles & Amphibians

**Written and Illustrated
by Todd Telander**

FALCONGUIDES

ESSEX, CONNECTICUT

FALCONGUIDES®

An imprint of The Globe Pequot Publishing Group, Inc.
64 South Main Street
Essex, CT 06426
www.globepequot.com

Falcon and FalconGuides are registered trademarks and Make Adventure Your Story is a trademark of The Globe Pequot Publishing Group, Inc.

Illustrations: Todd Telander
Project Editor: Staci Zacharski
Text Design: Sheryl P. Kober
Layout Artist: Sue Murray

Library of Congress Cataloging-in-Publication Data is available on file.

ISBN 978-0-7627-8192-8

To my wife, Kirsten, my children, Miles and Oliver, and my parents,
all of whom have supported and encouraged me through the years.

Contents

Reptiles

Amphibians

Introduction

Welcome to the world of reptiles and amphibians, an incredibly diverse group of primitive animals that range from the fierce crocodiles and venomous snakes to the generally docile salamanders and frogs. Misunderstood and unnoticed, herps (as they are collectively called) generally take a backseat to the more visible birds and mammals for wildlife enthusiasts. Perhaps because some herps are venomous, the group is feared as a whole. Yet with a little knowledge, caution, and patience, you will be safely rewarded with the beauty and mystery of these scaled, slimly, or bumpy friends.

Reptiles comprise the crocodilians, snakes, lizards, and turtles (in additions to some smaller groups). They are characterized by having dry, scaly skin, and an ectothermic metabolism, whereby they derive their body heat from external sources such as basking on rocks in the sun. Many burrow and hibernate in cold temperatures. They either bear live young or lay soft, leathery eggs in the ground. Amphibians (frogs, toads, and salamanders) are also ectotherms but typically have smooth, moist skin and are restricted to areas in or near water. They lay their eggs in water and undergo some form of (often dramatic) metamorphosis from juvenile to adult.

Within the United States there are more than 450 species of reptiles and amphibians, so this guide is meant to be a general overview, not a comprehensive study, of this diversity. It is an introduction to some of the most common and distinct species that call this land their home—and a starting place to your explorations of these fascinating creatures.

Notes about the Species Accounts

Names

Both the common name and the scientific name are included for each entry. Since common names tend to vary regionally, or there may be more than one common name for each species, the universally accepted scientific name of genus and species (such as *Dermochelys coriacea* for the Leatherback Sea Turtle) is more reliable to be certain of identification. Also, one can often learn interesting facts about an animal by the English translation of its Latin name. For instance, the genus name *Dermochelys* means "skin of a turtle," and *coriacea* means "of the nature of leather."

Size

Most size measurements refer to overall length, from nose tip to the end of the tail. For turtles, the measurement is the length of the shell (carapace) only; for frogs and toads, the measurement is from nose to tailbone (excluding leg length). Size may vary considerably within a species (because of age, sex, or environmental conditions), so use measurement as a general guide, not a rule. Also, many species of lizards easily lose their tail when attacked, so you may likely find differing overall lengths as the tail regenerates. Be aware that some field guides give sizes for lizards and salamanders that are only of the body length, without including the tail. Except for the American Alligator and American Crocodile, all sizes are provided in inches.

Range

This term refers to the geographical area where a species is likely to be found, such as the Southwest, Rocky Mountains, Southeast coastal plains, Pacific Ocean, etc. Some species may be found throughout their range, whereas others prefer very specific habitats within their range.

Habitat

An animal's habitat is one of the first clues to its identification. Note the environment (including vegetation, climate, elevation, substrate, presence or absence of water) where you see an animal, and compare it with the description listed. Some common habitats include woodlands, grassland, desert, lakes and ponds, swamps, sand dunes, open ocean, suburbs, and farmlands.

Illustrations

The illustrations show the adult animals in their most common coloration. Many species show variation among subspecies in different geographical areas, in different seasons, or between the sexes; these variations are described in the text.

Characteristics of the Major Groups of Reptiles and Amphibians

The following diagrams illustrate some of the principal characteristics of the major groups of reptiles and amphibians. I have, for the most part, used familiar language to describe the animals in this book, but there are occasions when it makes more sense to use some terms developed by the scientific community, especially when referring to body parts.

Crocodialians

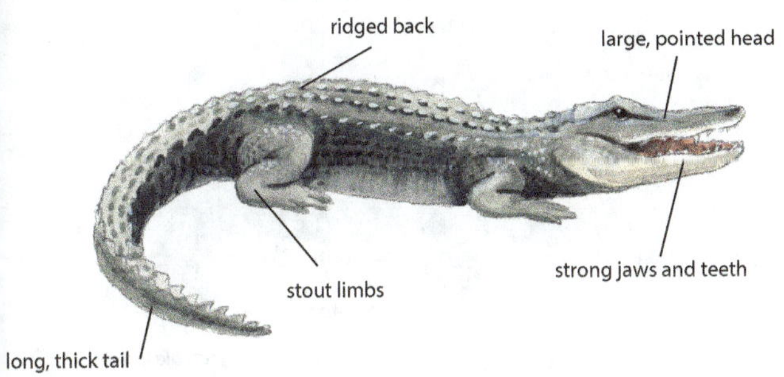

Lizards

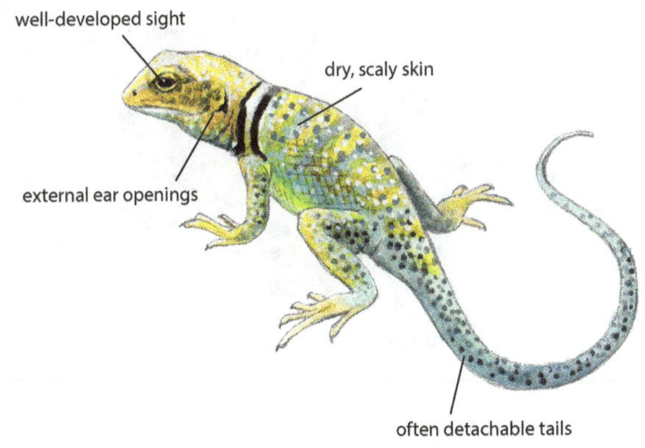

Snakes

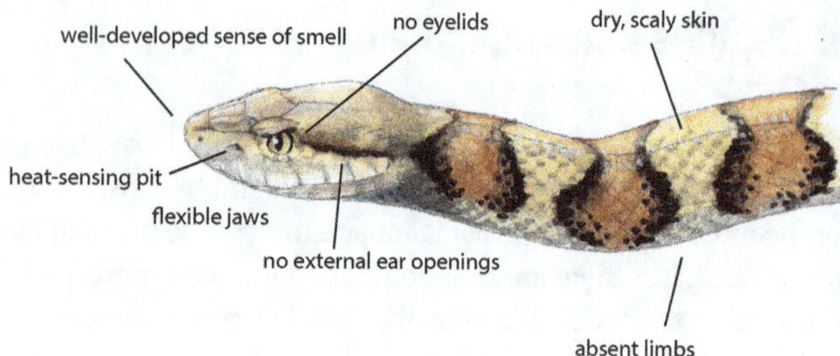

Turtles

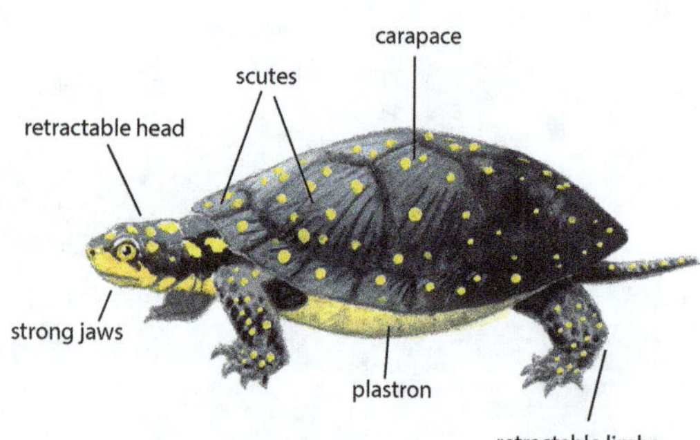

Frogs

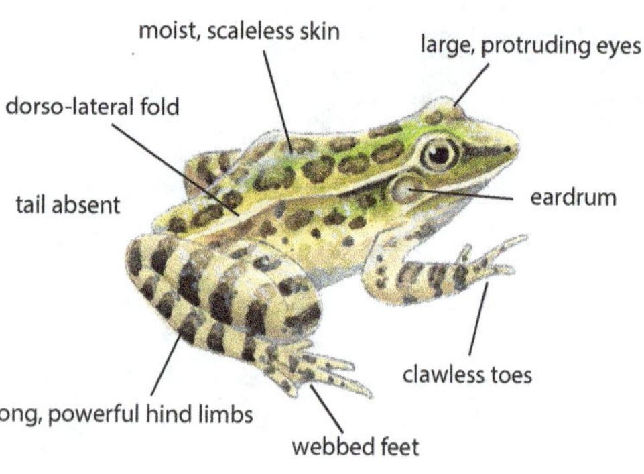

Toads

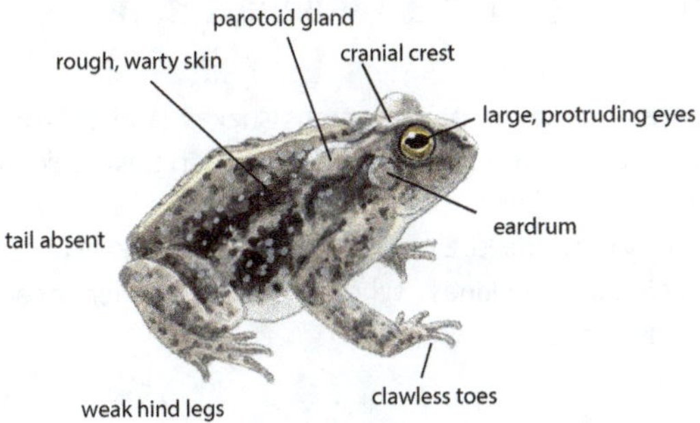

Salamanders

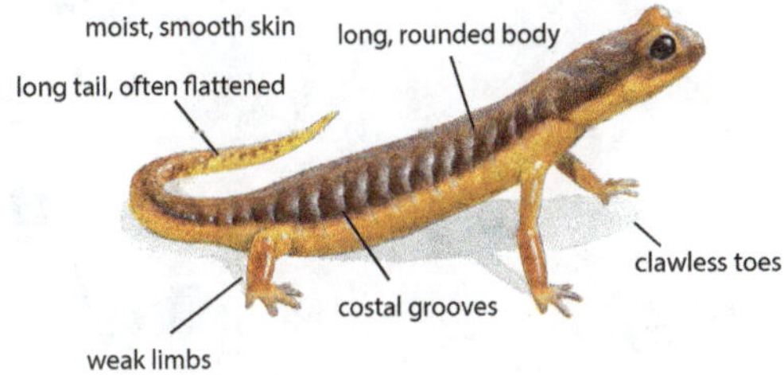

Caution Regarding Venomous Reptiles

Below are some of the venomous snakes (and the one lizard) found in the United States and described in this book. Although most snakes will flee from disturbance, others can be aggressive, especially if surprised. Even if not fatal, a bite is likely to cause considerable pain and illness. When in doubt, stay clear of any snake you cannot positively identify.

Eastern Diamondback Rattlesnake

Western Rattlesnake

Copperhead

Cottonmouth

Sidewinder

Gila Monster

Eastern Coral Snake

REPTILES

American Alligator, *Alligator mississippiensis*
Family Alligatoridae (alligators)
Size: Up to 12' long; males larger than females
Range: Southeastern United States and west to the Rio Grande in Texas
Habitat: Most aquatic environments; fresh or brackish swamps, mangroves

The American Alligator is the largest reptile in North America. Once threatened with extinction, it is now protected and maintaining stable populations. It is strong and compact, with a large, thick head with a rounded snout; short limbs; and imposing, teeth-laden jaws. The skin is lined with ridges along the back and colored gray to greenish above, paler underneath. Juveniles are black with pale, cream-colored bands. American Alligators are adept swimmers; they move slowly on land except for occasional rapid lunges. They are carnivores and will eat almost any available food, including fish, reptiles, birds, and mammals to the size of livestock.

American Crocodile, *Crocodylus acutus*
Family Crocodylidae (crocodiles)
Size: Up to 15' long
Range: Southern tip of Florida and the Keys
Habitat: Swamps, bogs, mangroves, salt marshes

The American Crocodile is an endangered, tropical species that within the United States is found only in the extreme southern portions of Florida. Its body is very large, with a long tail; thick, stubby legs; and a narrow, elongated snout. The scaled skin has raised ridges on the back and tail. It is colored grayish green, with irregular black bands across the body and tail, becoming less obvious in older individuals. With the mouth closed, the large teeth of the lower jaw are visible, unlike in alligators. American Crocodiles feed on fish, birds, amphibians, small mammals, and crabs and often rest with their mouths held open.

Texas Horned Lizard, *Phrynosoma cornutum*
Family Phrynosomatidae (horned lizards and allies)
Size: Up to 7" long
Range: Texas and surrounding regions, north to Kansas. Introduced in isolated regions of southeastern states
Habitat: Arid habitats with sparse vegetation

The Texas Horned Lizard is one of more than a dozen species of horned lizards (sometimes erroneously called "horned toads"), adapted to harsh, arid conditions and adorned with fearsome, pointed scales and horns. Its body is flattened, with a short, tapered tail, and is overall coarse and spiny. It has long central "crown" horns at the top of the head and two rows of fringed scales along the sides. The color is any variation of earth tones, with darker splotches behind the neck, on the back, and on the tail. A pale stripe runs down the center of the back, and dark lines radiate from the eyes. Texas Horned Lizards are active during the day, preying mostly on ants, termites, and other small insects. They find shelter by burrowing in loose soil or hiding beneath bushes and rocks.

Side-blotched Lizard, *Uta stansburiana*
Family Phrynosomatidae (horned lizards and allies)
Size: Up to 6" long
Range: Western United States; southern Washington to western Texas
Habitat: Dry, rocky, or sandy areas; grasslands; chaparral

The Side-blotched Lizard is a small, common lizard of arid western regions, with a long, tapered tail; long toes on the hind legs; external ear openings; and a distinct fold of skin on the throat (the gular fold). The color is generally brownish or gray, which can be uniform or interrupted with a variety of spots, stripes, or chevrons. There is a dark blue or black blotch on the sides of the body just behind the front legs, for which the lizard gets its name. Males also have gray and orange stripes on the throat and blue-gray speckling across the back and tail. They are active during the day, basking on rocks or logs and hopping or running among rocks, searching for small invertebrate prey, including insects and scorpions. The male is illustrated.

Eastern Fence Lizard, *Sceloporus undulatus*
Family Iguanidae (iguanid lizards)
Size: Up to 6" long
Range: Central and northern Florida
Habitat: A wide variety of sunny habitats; grasslands, woodlands, brushy areas

The Eastern Fence Lizard includes several subspecies of varying color patterns including grayish or brownish, with longitudinal striping, spotting, or a combination. In Florida, most individuals have dark, ragged bars across the back; males also show blue patches on the belly and chin. It is a compact, long-tailed lizard with big feet, a blunt face, and scaled, dry skin. Solitary and active during the day, fence lizards scurry through sheltered areas or among trees, feeding on all kinds of insects and other invertebrates.

Green Anole, *Anolis carolinensis*
Family Iguanidae (iguanid lizards)
Size: Up to 8" long
Range: Throughout Florida
Habitat: Virtually any habitat with trees, vines, or tall brush, including buildings and fences in urban areas

The Green Anole is a common, arboreal lizard that is often raised as a pet. It has a thin body, a long tail, a pointed snout, and padded toes to aid in climbing vertical surfaces. Its color can vary from bright green to brown or gray, depending on environmental factors or stress, but the undersides are always paler. Males develop an extendible, pinkish skin flap under the throat (the "throat fan"). Active during the day, Green Anoles often bask head down on tree branches, buildings, or fences. They forage with stealth and patience for their prey of insects and other invertebrates.

Chuckwalla, *Sauromalus obesus*
Family Iguanidae (iguanid lizards)
Size: Up to 16" long
Range: Far southwestern United States, including southern California
Habitat: Arid, rocky areas, especially near creosote bushes

The Chuckwalla is a large lizard of the desert, frequently seen basking in the sun atop boulders in temperatures of over 100 degrees Fahrenheit. Its common name is a Spanish interpretation of a native American name for this species, and the scientific name translates to bad, dismal lizard (probably due to its ominous appearance, because it is not poisonous). It has a wide belly and flattened back; a medium-length, blunt-tipped, rounded tail; and coarse granular scales. The skin is endowed with multiple wrinkles and folds, allowing this lizard to expand with air and lodge itself firmly into crevices to avoid predation. The body, head, and limbs are mostly black, with variable shades and speckling of red and white across the back and sides and a paler, yellowish tail. Females and juveniles often have distinct bands across the back and on the tail. Males have small pores on the inner part of the hind legs that secrete fluids to mark their territory. Chuckwallas rest at night in burrows, under rocks, or in crevices, becoming active at daytime. They are vegetarians, foraging for leaves, buds, flowers, and fruit, particularly from the creosote bush, but they will occasionally eat insects.

Species Fun Fact!

No meat for these critters! Chuckwallas live off of a strictly vegetarian diet.

Greater Earless Lizard, *Cophosaurus texanus*
Family Iguanidae (iguanid lizards)
Size: Up to 7" long
Range: Southwestern United States
Habitat: Open sandy or rocky ground in chaparral, scrub, open woodlands

The Greater Earless Lizard is a medium-size, speedy, desert-dwelling lizard with a long, flattened tail; very long hind toes; a short, triangular head; and smooth, granular scales. As its name implies, it lacks the external ear openings that are present in most lizards. It has an exquisite color and pattern, with a pale gray front end and head, orangey midsection, greenish hindquarters and lower belly with two black bands, and black bands on the underside of the tail. Females develop an orangey-pink throat during breeding season. It runs with its tail curved up, revealing the dark barring underneath, and uses the raised tail posture to defend itself against predators as well. The tail can be detached as a last defensive resort but will regenerate. Active during the day, Greater Earless Lizards often bask in the sun before scampering from rock to rock chasing their favored prey of insects and spiders.

Western Slender Glass Lizard, *Ophisaurus attenuatus*
Family Anguidae (glass and alligator lizards)
Size: Up to 40" long
Range: Central and southeastern United States
Habitat: Arid woodlands and fields

The Western Slender Glass Lizard is one of several members of leg-less lizards, superficially resembling snakes but having such non-snake features as a stiff body, eyelids, external ear openings, and a rigid jaw. Because of its stiff body, it has lateral grooves on either side of its body that allow it to expand for breathing and ingesting large prey. The color is pale brown with a thin, black dorsal stripe; white speckles along the sides; and black striping below the groove. It burrows at night and becomes active in the daytime, feeding on insects, small mammals, and eggs of birds or other reptiles. If attacked, it will squirm violently to escape and may detach its tail to distract predators, but the tail will regenerate.

Northern Alligator Lizard, *Elgaria coerulea*
Family Anguidae (glass and alligator lizards)
Size: Up to 12" long
Range: Pacific Northwest to coastal California and the Sierra Nevada
Habitat: Cool and moist woodlands or fields

The Northern Alligator Lizard has a stout body; a triangular head with a long snout; short limbs; and distinct grooves along each side of its body, allowing it to expand for breathing and feeding. The skin is greenish brown to bluish, with variable dark spots that may coalesce into bands or stripes. The belly is paler, with thin, dark stripes that run between the scales. Juveniles are very smooth (like a skink), with a wide, light stripe down the back and no dark bands. Alligator lizards are secretive, moving through and under logs, rock, and dense brush searching for insects, eggs, or small vertebrates. If captured, the lizard may detach its tail or emit feces.

Collared Lizard, *Crotaphytus collaris*
Family Crotaphytidae (collared and leopard lizards)
Size: Up to 14" long
Range: Great Basin and southwestern states
Habitat: Dry, rocky areas

Also known as the "mountain boomer," the Collared Lizard is a chunky, colorful lizard with a large head; large limbs; a long, narrow, rounded tail; and smooth, granular scales. Its most distinctive mark is a black-and-white collar band on the back of the neck. Otherwise the color and patterning are quite variable but usually yellowish, tan, or blue-green with small spots on the body, tail, legs, and face, and light banding across the back. Breeding females show orange markings along the sides. Collared Lizards leap from rock to rock or run on the open ground on their hind legs with tail raised, looking like a quick little dinosaur. To feed, it ambushes smaller lizards and insects, which it subdues with powerful jaws.

Long-nosed Leopard Lizard, *Gambelia wislizenii*
Family Crotaphytidae (collared and leopard lizards)
Size: Up to 15" long
Range: Great Basin and southwestern states
Habitat: Arid, sandy, or gravelly areas with sparse vegetation

The Long-nosed Leopard Lizard is a fairly large, agile, stout lizard with a large head and limbs and a long, rounded tail (sometimes reaching twice the length of the body). The snout is long, and the scales are smooth and granular. The closely related Blunt-nosed Leopard Lizard has a short, blunt snout. The color is brown to gray above, paler below, with variable markings depending on region and subspecies (of which four or five are recognized). In general there are light crossbars along the back and an overall speck-ling of dark brown "leopard spots" on the tail, head, and body. These spots can be round, squarish, fragmented, and sometimes bordered by whitish rings. In cool temperatures the skin may become noticeably darker; during breeding, males develop reddish bellies, while females have reddish markings on the sides. The belly is mostly unmarked pale gray. Active during the day, often hiding in the shade of brush or rocks, Long-nosed Leopard Lizards scamper out quickly along the ground, preying on insects, other lizards, or even small mammals. They breed during the summer, and in colder months they hibernate in the safety of burrows. When running fast, they may lift their front legs off the ground in a bipedal manner. Although not poisonous, they have powerful jaws and can inflict a painful bite.

Species Fun Fact!

The skin on Long-nosed Leopard Lizards can change color and shades depending on dips in the temperature or during breeding season.

Mediterranean House Gecko, *Hemidactylus turcicus*
Family Gekkonidae (geckos)
Size: Up to 5" long
Range: Throughout southeastern United States
Habitat: Developed areas, walls of buildings, trees; lights at night

The Mediterranean House Gecko is a species native to the Mediterranean region that has been introduced to the southern United States and maintains a stable or growing population. It has a large head with a rounded snout, eyes that are lidless and have vertical pupils, and feet with adhesive pads to aid in climbing vertical surfaces. The skin color can range from pale gray to brownish or tan with dark spots (colors are usually palest at night). The body is covered with rough, whitish bumps. Most active at night, Mediterranean House Geckos feed on moths and other insects by waiting quietly, then snatching up prey as it draws near. They make a high-pitched squeak or chirp, somewhat like a mouse or a small bird.

Western Banded Gecko, *Coleonyx variegatus*
Family Gekkonidae (geckos)
Size: Up to 6" long
Range: Far Southwest and Southern California
Habitat: Arid, rocky areas; sand dunes; chaparral

The Western Banded Gecko is suited to extreme desert habitats. It is a medium-size lizard with soft, bumpy skin; a large head; vertical pupils in protruding eyes; thin, short toes; and a plump, rounded tail. The overall color is light brown or pinkish, with dark brown, broken crossbars and spots on the back, sides, and head, sometimes forming more distinct bands on the tail; the underside is whitish. Juveniles have more complete banding on the body, which tends to break up as the lizard ages. Western Banded Geckos remain under rocks, logs, or in crevices during the heat of day, becoming active at night. They feed on insects and other invertebrates, habitually quivering their tails in preparation for a lurch at prey. There is a constriction at the base of the tail, where it may detach if the lizard is attacked.

Gila Monster, *Heloderma suspectum*
Family Helodermatidae (Gila monster)
Size: Up to 24" long
Range: Arizona, southern Nevada, Mojave Desert
Habitat: Arid, gravelly areas, often near a water source and sparse vegetation

The only venomous lizard in the United States, the Gila Monster is a very large, stocky lizard with a thick body, blunt head, and a short, rounded tail. The tough, nonoverlapping scales resemble a tapestry of small, smooth beads. The color is a variable pattern of contrasting black and yellow-orange bands and spots, with a black face. It rests in burrows or under rocks during the day and becomes active at night, searching for food such as small mammals, birds, and eggs, climbing trees if necessary and using its snakelike tongue to smell and taste the trail of its prey. Gila Monsters have a powerful bite and secrete poison. Although bites to humans are rare, it is best to avoid handling them.

Five-lined Skink, *Plestiodon fasciatus*
Family Scincidae (skinks)
Size: Up to 8" long
Range: Eastern United States
Habitat: Moist woodlands

Skinks in general have long, slender, cylindrical bodies; long tapering tails; smooth scales; and small limbs. The Five-lined Skink is a common eastern skink that is overall black, with five thin yellow stripes running the length of the body (the stripes often fade with age). The tail is gray except in juveniles, which display a bright blue tail. Breeding males have a bright, rusty-orange face. Active during the day, Five-lined Skinks bask on tree trunks or rocks or lurk among leaf litter, rotten logs, and rocks foraging for insects, worms, snails, or small mammals. If attacked, they may detach their tail to distract predators.

Mole Skink, *Plestiodon egregius*
Family Scincidae (skinks)
Size: Up to 6" long
Range: Far southeastern United States, including Florida, Alabama, and Louisiana
Habitat: Sandy areas, dunes, beaches

Named for its habit of burrowing in loose, sandy soils, the Mole Skink is also found in moist areas under rocks, stumps, and leaf litter. It is a long-bodied, cylindrical lizard with a long, tapered tail; small limbs; thick neck; and smooth, shiny scales. The color is brownish or grayish overall, with two pale stripes running along either side of the back. The tail color varies depending on region and can be bright blue, reddish, orange, or violet. Breeding males develop orange markings on the chin and belly. Mole Skinks feed on ground-dwelling or tunneling insects, spiders, and other invertebrates. Wary and quick, it will detach its tail readily if attacked.

Western Skink, *Plestiodon skiltonianus*
Family Scincidae (skinks)
Size: Up to 9" long
Range: West of the Rocky Mountains, Canada to southern California
Habitat: A wide variety of habitats, including woodlands, streamsides, and fields

Like the other skinks, the Western Skink has a long, narrow, cylindrical body; a long, tapering tail; small limbs; and smooth, shiny scales. It is distinctively colored, with a broad brown stripe down the back, blackish stripes along the sides, and pale stripes between these. The tail is bright blue in juveniles, becoming grayish in mature individuals. Breeding males develop orange markings under the chin and on the belly. Active during the day, Western Skinks usually stay hidden under leaves, rocks, or stumps. They feed on insects, spiders, sowbugs, earthworms, and other invertebrates. They will dig burrows and remain there for winter in cold climates.

Western Whiptail, *Cnemidophorus tigris*
Family Teiidae (whiptails and racerunners)
Size: Up to 12" long
Range: Great Basin region, California, south to western Texas
Habitat: Arid, open areas; open woodlands

Whiptails are known for their quick and jerky movements; relatively long, slender bodies; large limbs; and long, thin, whiplike tails. There are prominent external ear openings, and the eyes are oval and tapered at each corner. The scales of the belly are large and squarish, while those of the back are rounded and granular; the front of the limbs also show enlarged, smooth scales, and the tail has scales that are ridged. Of the Western Whiptail, several subspecies exist with variations in color and pattern, but all generally show dark spotting or marbling on the head and body over a grayish, yellowish, or brownish background, with several paler longitudinal stripes down the back and sides (like tiger stripes, and hence the scientific name *tigris*). The belly and throat are normally whitish to pale yellow but in some cases may be nearly black. The tail is blue in juveniles, fading to pale gray in adults. Juveniles are also more brightly colored than adults. Active during the day, Western Whiptails commonly flick out their tongues to sense for smells, and feed on insects and spiders in leaf litter or underground. Wary by nature, they run rapidly to avoid danger, often seeking the protection of brush or burrows, and will detach their tails if attacked, which are later regenerated. Curiously, some populations of whiptails consist entirely of females, which are able to reproduce without fertilization, creating communities of clones.

Species Fun Fact!

The long, thin tail of these critters isn't the only thing that gets whipped about. Western Whiptails whip out their tongues to sense for smells, too.

Six-lined Racerunner, *Cnemidophorus sexlineatus*
Family Teiidae (whiptails and racerunners)
Size: Up to 10" long
Range: Lower latitude states east of the Rocky Mountains
Habitat: Fields with sparse vegetation, open woodlands, rocky areas, streamsides

Closely related to the Western Whiptail, the Six-lined Racerunner has the same long, narrow body; long limbs; and very long, thin, whiplike tail. The body is lined with alternating yellowish or whitish stripes and brown to black stripes, often with a brown stripe along the middle of the back. The underparts are white in females, while males show a blue-green wash on the belly, foreparts, and throat. The tail is blue in juveniles and brownish in adults. Active in the daytime, Six-lined Racerunners bask in the sun and feed on insects and other invertebrates. They are very quick and agile, using speed to avoid capture. They burrow during colder temperatures.

Desert Night Lizard, *Xantusia vigilis*
Family Xantusidae (night lizards)
Size: Up to 6" long
Range: Far southwestern United States
Habitat: Arid sagebrush, desert, yucca habitats, pine-oak woodlands

The Desert Night Lizard is a small, secretive, slender lizard with a relatively large head; vertical pupils; a long, tapered tail; and soft scales, giving it a superficial appearance of a gecko. The color is light brown, olive, or grayish, with variable amounts of pale to distinct darker spots that often form longitudinal stripes along the back and sides. Contrary to their name, Desert Night Lizards are primarily active during the day but can also be active at twilight and nighttime during warmer weather. They lurk in the cover of fallen vegetation, rocks, and logs and feed on insects, larvae, and other invertebrates. They readily detach their tails if attacked.

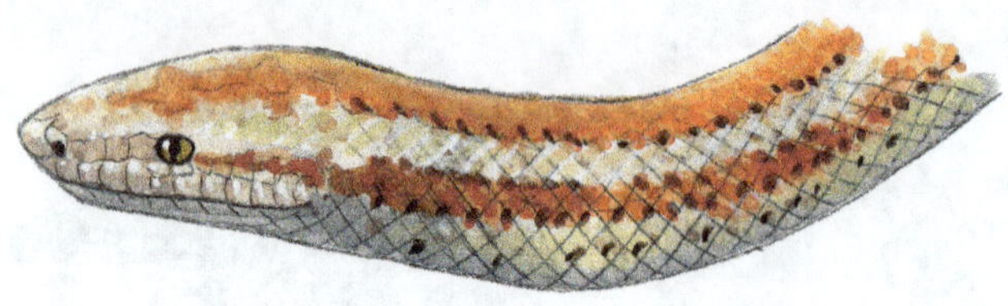

Rosy Boa, *Lichanura trivirgata*
Family Boidae (boas)
Size: Up to 40" long
Range: Southern California and southwestern Arizona
Habitat: Desert, arid rocky areas with sparse scrub

One of two species of native boas in the United States, the Rosy Boa is a stout, muscular snake with a head only slightly wider than the body; a blunt tail tip; vertical pupils; and smooth, glossy scales. The color is light gray, yellow-brown, or rosy, with three broad brown stripes running down the back and sides. Depending on the region, these stripes may be distinct or broken into irregular spots. Mostly nocturnal, Rosy Boas spend the day in crevices or under rocks. Docile by nature and popular as pets, they rarely bite but instead use constriction to suffocate and subdue their prey of small rodents and birds.

Rubber Boa, *Charina bottae*
Family Boidae (boas)
Size: Up to 30" long
Range: Pacific Northwest, extending to northern California, Nevada, and western Montana
Habitat: A wide variety of habitats, including woodlands, meadows, and streamsides

In addition to the Rosy Boa, the Rubber Boa is the only other boa native to the United States, preferring cool, moist conditions. It has a stout, muscular body; tiny eyes with vertical pupils; a small, blunt head; and a thick, blunt tail tip that resembles another head. The scales are small, sleek, and smooth, giving the appearance of rubber. The color is unmarked brown, reddish, or greenish gray above and yellow along the underside. Secretive and docile, the Rubber Boa will burrow or hide under leaves, rocks, or rotten wood. It will curl into a ball with its head buried and tail exposed when provoked, almost never biting as a defense. Active during night or twilight, it moves on the ground or in trees, or it swims. It uses constriction to subdue its prey of shrews, other small mammals, and birds; it also eats eggs.

Northern Water Snake, *Nerodia sipedon*
Family Colubridae (colubrid snakes)
Size: Up to 50" long
Range: Throughout central and eastern United States, except Florida
Habitat: Most freshwater habitats; streams, lakes, swamps

The Northern Water Snake is a highly aquatic, thick-bodied snake quite common in its range and never found far from water. Its color is highly variable but is usually light to dark brown or gray, with broad, darker brown, black, or reddish bands behind the neck and broken bands or mottling along the rest of the body. The underside is paler, often with crescent-shaped markings. Older snakes become nearly black overall. Active at all times of the day and night, it basks on rocks and logs near water or pursues all manner of aquatic prey, including frogs, minnows, salamanders, and crayfish. Although not venomous, water snakes are aggressive. If provoked, they will release a foul-smelling substance and can give a painful bite; because of an anticoagulant released in the bite, wounds may bleed profusely. Uncommon among snakes, they give birth to live young (sometimes over 50), who fend for themselves as soon as they are born. Where their ranges overlap, Northern Water Snakes can be mistaken for the venomous Cottonmouth, or Water Moccasin, which has a triangle-shaped head, vertical pupils, bands that usually encircle the body along its entire length, and no crescents on the belly.

Species Fun Fact!

Talk about big families! The Northern Water Snake can give birth to over 50 live young. Thankfully for the parents, these young can fend for themselves as soon as they are born.

Common Kingsnake, *Lampropeltis getulus*
Family Colubridae (colubrid snakes)
Size: Up to 72" long
Range: Throughout the southern half of the United States
Habitat: Quite varied, depending on region; desert, woodlands, wetlands, grasslands

The Common Kingsnake is a large, attractive, boldly-patterned snake with several subspecies across the United States. All have shiny scales and some version of dark and light banding or mottling, which is composed of yellows, blacks, or browns. Some individuals are mostly dark, with sparse, lighter speckles. Usually active during the day, or at night in warm weather, Common Kingsnakes feed on a wide variety of prey, including small mammals, birds, and even other snakes, which they kill by constriction. Kingsnakes are so named because, although nonvenomous, they prey on venomous snakes without consequence, being mostly immune to their bites.

Long-nosed Snake, *Rhinocheilus lecontei*
Family Colubridae (colubrid snakes)
Size: Up to 40" long
Range: Southwestern United States; California to Texas
Habitat: Arid grasslands, scrubland, chaparral

The Long-nosed Snake is a medium-size, thin, smooth-scaled snake of desert and semiarid regions of the Southwest and Great Basin. The head is scarcely wider than the body, and the snout is pointed with a countersunk lower jaw. The color varies regionally but in general is creamy yellow with broad black saddles speckled with lighter color, reddish coloring between these saddles, and black speckling on the sides. Some varieties lack the reddish color, being only black and creamy white. They keep under rocks or in underground burrows during the day, venturing out at night to hunt for small reptiles, eggs, mammals, and insects. In winter months they hibernate underground. If alarmed, they will assume a defensive posture in which the body coils and writhes, the tail quivers, and fluids are emitted from the anus.

Queen Snake, *Regina septemvittata*
Family Colubridae (colubrid snakes)
Size: Up to 36" long (females larger than males)
Range: Inland eastern United States; Great Lakes to the Gulf Coast
Habitat: Rocky or sandy streams and lakes, adjacent shorelines

The Queen Snake is a small to medium-size snake with a slender body; thin head; and rough, ridged scales. The color ranges from tan, brown, and olive-brown to nearly black, with a conspicuous pale yellow stripe running the length of each side and continuing along the lower half of the face. The belly is pale yellow, with two ventral and two lateral dark stripes. Sometimes thin, darker stripes can be seen on the back as well. Queen Snakes are primarily active during the day but can also be seen at night during periods of warm weather. They lurk among the grasses and rocks of shorelines and use their excellent swimming ability to hunt for newly-molted crayfish, their principal food.

Scarlet Snake, *Cemophora coccinea*
Family Colubridae (colubrid snakes)
Size: Up to 24" long
Range: Throughout the southeastern United States
Habitat: Dry hardwood or pine woodlands with sandy or loose soils

The Scarlet Snake is a relatively small, harmless snake with smooth, shiny scales; a small head; and a pointed snout. The color is whitish to creamy yellow, with broad, black-bordered red saddles along the back and sides that do not encircle the body. The belly is unmarked whitish, creamy, or gray. Scarlet Snakes can be distinguished from the venomous coral snake by their red snout (not black) and the dark patterning, with the red and yellowish bands always separated by black. They spend the daytime in underground burrows or under rocks, logs, and leaf litter, emerging at night to hunt for reptiles and their eggs, amphibians, and small mammals.

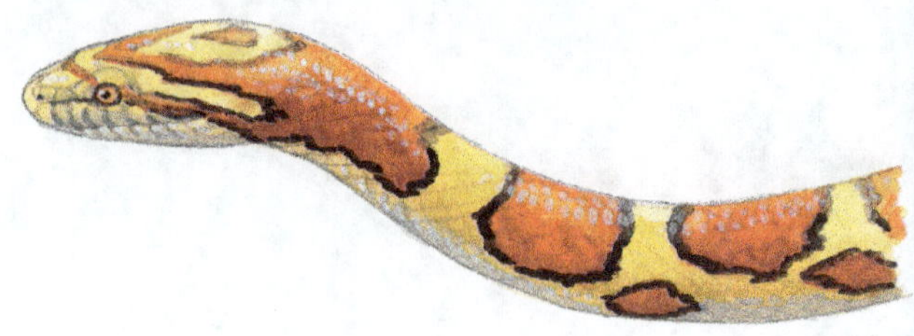

Corn Snake, *Elaphe guttata*
Family Colubridae (colubrid snakes)
Size: Up to 72" long
Range: Central and southeastern United States
Habitat: Quite variable; streamsides, woodlands, rocky slopes, farmlands

Also known as the Red Rat Snake, the Corn Snake is a handsome, long-bodied snake with a docile disposition; it is popular in the pet trade. Eastern individuals are brownish yellow, with dark-bordered orange or reddish saddle-like marks down the back and smaller marks along the sides. Farther west, the background color is more grayish, with brown marks. In all varieties the underside is paler, with dark speckles; the top of the head usually sports a pointed mark between the eyes and a dark stripe from the eye to the base of the jaw. There are two dark stripes on the underside of the tail. Staying in burrows, crevices, or under rocks at night, Corn Snakes are excellent climbers, and can be found during the day or night (principally night in warmer months) searching for small mammals, birds, bats, and reptiles, which they subdue by constriction. They also spend time in underground burrows where they prey on rodents. The common name comes from the fact that they are familiar near corn storage areas, attracted to the rodents that feed there. The Corn Snake can be confused with the venomous Copperhead Snake, which has a wider head, facial pit, plain colored forehead, and bands that are constricted on the back like an hourglass.

Species Fun Fact!

The Corn Snake's name comes from the area in which it is commonly found—near corn. The snake often follows its prey, the rodent (which feeds off of the corn) to the area.

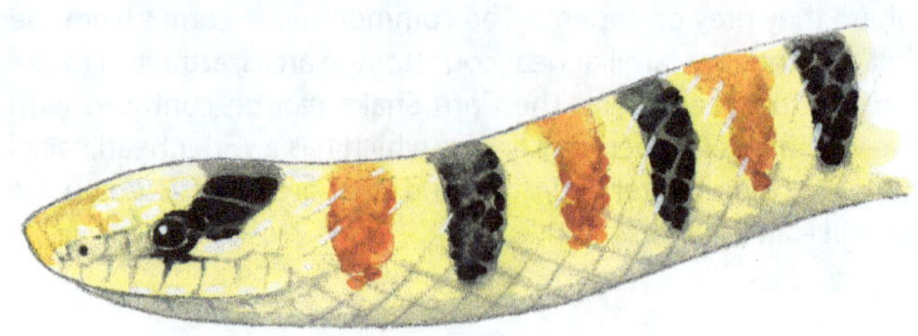

Western Shovel-nosed Snake, *Chionactis occipitalis*
Family Colubridae (colubrid snakes)
Size: Up to 16" long
Range: Far southwestern United States; southern Nevada to Mexico
Habitat: Sandy areas of desert, arid scrub, rocky slopes

The small Western Shovel-nosed Snake is restricted to areas of loose sand and gravel in which it deftly glides through and borrows into. The body is covered with smooth, glossy scales, colored whitish to creamy yellow, with fewer than twenty-one black bands or saddles and sometimes with reddish-orange saddles in between. A black mask on the top of the head extends between the eyes. The snout is flattened with and overriding upper jaw, giving it the "shovel-nosed" appearance. The eyes are dark and non-protruding, and the belly is somewhat concave. It is active during the night or at twilight searching for insects, spiders, and scorpions.

Striped Whipsnake, *Masticophis taeniatus*
Family Colubridae (colubrid snakes)
Size: Up to 72" long
Range: Great Basin region from central Washington to Texas
Habitat: Deserts, sageland, rocky areas, mountains, grasslands

Related to the racers, the Striped Whipsnake is aggressive and speedy. Its body is long and thin, like a bullwhip, with a narrow, tapering tail; smooth scales; and large, round eyes. The color is brownish, gray, or nearly black above, with two pale yellow or white stripes along each side, along with a broken or solid thin, dark stripe in between. The underside is whitish, pale pink, or yellowish. Active during the day, the snake moves along the ground or in trees, feeding on other reptiles, small mammals, insects, and birds. It hibernates during cold weather in burrows or under rocks. Striped Whipsnakes usually speed away into the brush or rocks if provoked, and although not venomous, they will readily bite.

Gopher Snake, *Pituophis melanoleucus*
Family Colubridae (colubrid snakes)
Size: 48"–96" long
Range: Throughout most of the United States
Habitat: Desert, pine-oak woodlands, rocky areas, scrubland, prairies

The Gopher Snake is a widespread, large, powerful snake that has more than a dozen subspecies and goes by many common names, including pine snake, pine-gopher, and bullsnake. Its body is thick, with ridged scales on the upper surface; the eyes have round pupils. The base color is light brown, pale gray, or yellowish, heavily marked with reddish-brown or blackish blotches and spots. Some varieties are nearly solid black; others have distinct, lengthwise stripes. Chiefly active during the day, Gopher Snakes hide in rodent or tortoise burrows, crevices, or under rocks during the day but often are found during the night in warm weather. They hunt on the ground, in trees, or in burrows for rodents and other reptiles, leaping at their prey and constricting it with their strong bodies. If confronted, they will flatten their heads, hiss, and quiver their tails.

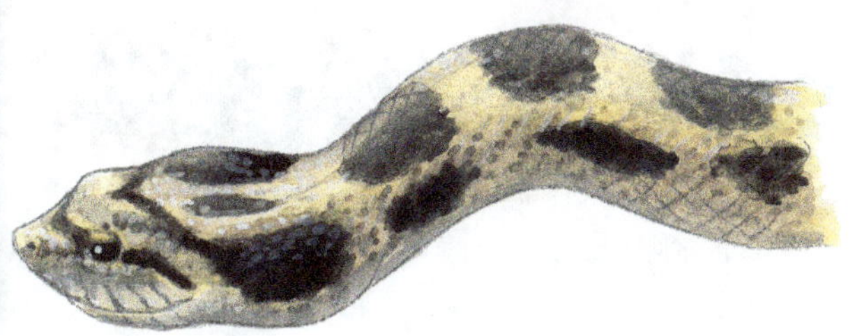

Eastern Hognose Snake, *Heterodon platyrhinos*
Family Colubridae (colubrid snakes)
Size: Up to 40" long
Range: Throughout the eastern United States
Habitat: Prairies, open woodlands with loose soils, farmlands

Also known as the Puff Adder or Blow Viper, the Eastern Hognose Snake is a widespread snake with a thick body, wide neck, large eyes, and a characteristic upturned snout. The color is quite variable but is usually some shade of yellow, tan, brown, or red, with irregular dark brown or black blotches on the back and sides, although some individuals may be uniformly dark. The undersides are paler, especially on the tail. Active during the day, Eastern Hognose Snakes retreat to underground burrows during periods of cool or very warm weather. They feed on a wide variety of small mammals, birds, reptiles, and amphibians, which they hunt on the ground or in burrows. Although relatively harmless to humans, they perform a dramatic defensive display of hissing and puffing up the neck to look larger, or they may play dead.

Ringneck Snake, *Diadophis punctatus*
Family Colubridae (colubrid snakes)
Size: Up to 30" long
Range: Throughout most of the United States except the north-central states
Habitat: Quite varied; mostly moist areas in woodlands, fields, scrub, and streamsides

The Ringneck Snake is a small, thin, smooth snake comprising a dozen or so subspecies found across the United States. All varieties are characterized by a uniform gray to brownish upper surface, a bright yellow-orange or red underside (brightest on the tail), a dark head, and a conspicuous yellow-orange neck ring. The neck ring may be complete or broken; the belly is often marked with black spots. Secretive, Ringneck Snakes keep to moist areas of their habitat with cover of rocks, leaf litter, rotting stumps, and burrows. They feed on small prey such as insects, worms, and small vertebrates. A common defense posture includes lifting its front parts, supported by a coiled rear, to expose the bright underside.

Racer, *Coluber constrictor*
Family Colubridae (colubrid snakes)
Size: Up to 60" long
Range: Throughout the United States except most of the Southwest
Habitat: Brush and thickets, often near water; suburbs

Comprising nearly a dozen subspecies, each with a different coloration, the Racer is a long, thin, speedy snake that is often sighted in residential areas. The eyes are dark and relatively large, the neck is thin, and the scales are smooth. Its color can be black, dark gray, bluish green, or brownish above and paler below, often with a whitish throat area. Young snakes are paler overall, with rounded, brownish spots along the back. Burrowing during the night, Racers are most active in the daytime, foraging on the ground for insects and small vertebrates, and are capable of climbing trees to escape danger. Although not venomous, they are capable of inflicting a painful bite.

Rough Green Snake, *Opeodrys aestivus*
Family Colubridae (colubrid snakes)
Size: Up to 45"
Range: Southeastern United States
Habitat: Brushy areas near water, swamps; trees, vines

The Rough Green Snake is a lithe and graceful snake that prefers a life aboveground, slithering though branches and vines near water. It is small and narrow with a small head and has scales with thin ridges along their centers (keeled). Adults are well camouflaged in leafy vegetation, being unmarked yellow-green above and on the sides and white or pale yellow along the belly and lower face. Juveniles are grayish green. Rough Green Snakes are most active during the day, foraging for insects and spiders, which they swallow whole after stealthily pursuing and striking. Their large eyes aid in the detection of the smallest movements of their prey. They are not aggressive, and will retreat into the brush or use their excellent swimming ability to enter the water to escape danger. At night, they can be found in a coiled posture in the nooks of tree branches or in leaf litter, and during cold months will hibernate. Females, when preparing to lay eggs, will retreat to moist areas away from standing water, but they and the young will soon return to the wetlands. The similar Smooth Green Snake has smooth scales and is found in the western, midwestern and northeastern United States.

Species Fun Fact!

The Rough Green Snake differs from its cousin, the Smooth Green Snake, in the ridged scales that line its body.

Common Garter Snake, *Thamnophis sirtalis*
Family Colubridae (colubrid snakes)
Size: Up to 40" long
Range: Throughout the United States
Habitat: Well-vegetated areas near water, marshes; urban parks

The Common Garter Snake is, true to its name, a widespread and common snake with more than ten subspecies that commonly frequents developed areas and home gardens. It is a thin, medium-size snake with a head slightly wider that the body and relatively large eyes. The skin has keeled scales and is extremely variable in color, depending on subspecies, but always showing three longitudinal stripes—one running across the top to the back and two along the sides. Often there are blackish spots between the stripes. The underparts are pale. Garter snakes freely move from land to water; they feed on insects, aquatic invertebrates, fish, and small mammals. They are relatively harmless but can bite and may emit foul-smelling fluid if trapped.

Milk Snake, *Lampropeltis triangulum*
Family Colubridae (colubrid snakes)
Size: Up to 60" long
Range: Throughout the eastern United States; west into the Rocky Mountains
Habitat: Highly variable depending on region; forests, fields, wetlands, streamsides, farmland

One of the most widespread snakes in the United States, the Milk Snake is narrow bodied, with a small head and smooth scales. There is much geographical variation in color and pattern, but generally there are black-bordered reddish or brown bands or blotches over a yellowish, tan, or pale gray background. The lighter background color is widest toward the base; in many cases there is a V-shaped mark on the top of the head, and the belly may have a distinct black-and-white pattern. Active day or night, favoring covered areas under logs or in rocks, Milk Snakes prey on small mammals, eggs, and other reptiles, subduing them by constriction and suffocation. The common name is derived from the myth that they suck the milk of cows.

Eastern Coral Snake, *Micrurus fulvius*
Family Elapidae (elapid snakes)
Size: Up to 24" or longer
Range: Southeastern United States
Habitat: Woodlands near water, rural gardens, hammocks

The Eastern Coral Snake is generally secretive in nature, but caution is advised, as its bite is venomous and can be fatal. Its body is slender, with smooth, shiny scales and a small, blunt-tipped head (the head is no wider than the body). The color is striking, with wide red and black bands separated by thinner yellow bands. The head is black, with a wide yellow band just behind the eyes. Many harmless snakes have similar colors, but one distinguishing mark of the Coral Snake is that the red and yellow bands are always adjacent to one another. Coral Snakes move through dense leaf litter and fallen wood, feeding on smaller snakes, other reptiles, and amphibians.

Western Blind Snake, *Leptotyphlops humilis*
Family Leptotyphlopidae (slender blind snakes)
Size: Up to 16" long
Range: Far southwestern United States; from Southern California and Nevada into western Texas
Habitat: Areas of loose, sandy soils; desert, chaparral, rocky slopes

Blind snakes, also known as worm snakes, have thin, cylindrical bodies with blunt tails, small mouths, smooth scales, and nearly uniform width along the length of the body. They have only vestigial eyes and are virtually blind (although they can sense light and dark), having small dark spots where normal eyes would be. The Western Blind Snake is unmarked, colored grayish, pinkish, or brownish. There is also a small spine at the tip of the tail. It remains in crevices between rocks, in vegetation, or in burrows during the day, becoming active at night to hunt for insects, especially ants, termites, and millipedes, resisting stings with its tough scales.

Copperhead, *Agkistrodon contortrix*
Family Viperidae (pit vipers)
Size: Up to 60" long
Range: Eastern United States
Habitat: Woodlands, swamps, wetlands, rocky slopes

The Copperhead is a venomous pit viper with a thick body; a tapered tail; a large, triangular head that is clearly wider than the neck; vertical pupils; and heat-sensing pits between the eyes and nostrils. Depending on the subspecies, the color is some shade of earthy orange, olive, brown, or copper, with darker, reddish-brown bands along the body that are thin on top and wider on the sides. Juveniles have a yellowish tail. Copperheads are active during the day or night, depending on temperature, and seek dens in colder months. Well camouflaged, the snake lurks through rocks, brush, and logs, feeding on a variety of small vertebrates and insects, seizing its prey with long, retractable, venom-laden fangs. Caution is advised—Copperheads are aggressive, and bites can be fatal.

Sidewinder, *Crotalus cerastes*
Family Viperidae (pit vipers)
Size: Up to 31" long
Range: Southern Nevada, California, Arizona
Habitat: Desert, arid mountains

The Sidewinder is a relatively small, rough-scaled rattlesnake. It has the pit viper traits of a stout body; wide, triangular, flat head; vertical pupils; and heat-sensing pits between the eyes and nostrils. It is also known as the horned rattlesnake because of the enlarged, pointed scales just above the eyes, which can be lowered to protect the eyes. The color is quite pale overall—some shade of cryptic gray, tan, or brown—with many small patches of darker color. Often a dark line is seen behind the eyes. Mostly active at night or during twilight hours, Sidewinders otherwise hide in dens, vegetation, rocks, or burrows made by mammals. To feed, the snake awaits prey such as small mammals and lizards and then quickly attacks using long fangs and venom. The common name comes from the way this snake speeds over sandy and fine soils with a sideways, undulating movement.

Eastern Diamondback Rattlesnake, *Crotalus adamanteus*

Family Viperidae (pit vipers)
Size: Up to 72" long (or larger)
Range: Southeastern coastal plains
Habitat: Oak and pine woodlands, sandhills, swamps, prairies

The Eastern Diamondback Rattlesnake is North America's most massive snake and is highly venomous. The body is robust and long, with well-developed rattles at the tip of the tail (made of segmented, horny tissue). The large head is large, flared into a triangular shape, flattened on top, with dark eyes and a pronounced, heat-sensing pit. It also has a distinct dark stripe from the eyes to the base of the jaw. The body color is brownish, tan, or grayish, with many light-bordered diamond-shaped markings along the back, becoming more like bands on the tail. The underside is pale yellow with some diffuse spotting. This rattlesnake seeks shelter in burrows made by rodents and gopher tortoises or in the hollows of fallen trees, emerging during twilight hours to hunt. It actively pursues prey or waits in seclusion for an ambush, striking out at birds or mammals to the size of rabbits. From a coiled position with its head raised, it quickly snaps toward its victim, injecting venom through its hollow, retractable fangs. Although it usually chooses to flee when alarmed, it will readily stand its ground if there is an imminent threat. Extreme caution is advised around these snakes; bites can cause extreme pain and death in humans. It is quite similar to the Western Rattlesnake of southwestern North America, but their ranges do not overlap.

Species Fun Fact!

The most massive snake in North America, the Eastern Diamondback Rattlesnake can hunt and kill prey up to the size of a rabbit.

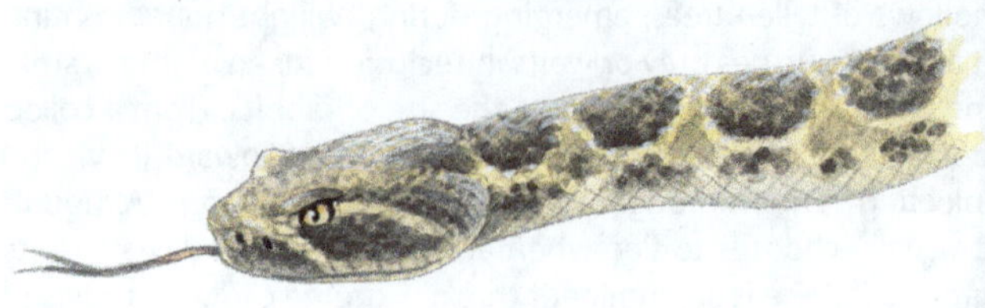

Western Rattlesnake, *Crotalus viridis*
Family Viperidae (pit vipers)
Size: Up to 62" long
Range: Throughout most of western United States
Habitat: Quite variable depending on region; forests, sand dunes, grasslands, rocky areas up to timberline

The Western Rattlesnake is a thick, rough-scaled, venomous pit viper with a flat, wide, triangular head; retractable fangs; and a tail tipped with horny segments that buzz when shaken. This species comprises several subspecies with variable coloration and size. The background color can be pale yellow, brown, reddish, greenish, or dark gray, with darker, light-edged blotches along the back that merge to cross bands on the tail. There is usually a pale stripe extending from the eye to the corner of the mouth. Western Rattlesnakes are active most of the day except in very hot weather, when they retreat into burrows made by mammals. They feed on small mammals, reptiles, and amphibians, striking and biting the prey, letting the venom kill the victim, and later ingesting it. Much caution is advised around these snakes; although they usually avoid humans, if surprised they can cause a painful or lethal bite.

Cottonmouth, *Agkistrodon piscivorus*

Family Viperidae (pit vipers)
Size: Up to 72" long
Range: Southeastern United States
Habitat: Swamps, lakes, streams, wetlands

Also known as the Water Moccasin, the Cottonmouth is a mostly aquatic snake that deserves much caution, as its bite can be fatal. It is a large, thick snake with a head noticeably wider than the body and an abruptly tapering tail. The color is variably blackish to greenish brown, paler below, with younger individuals showing ragged, lighter bands. There is a dark, light-bordered patch behind the eyes, and the inside of the mouth is whitish (giving the common name). As a member of the pit viper family, it has heat-sensing pits between the eyes and nostrils. Mostly nocturnal, Cottonmouths feed on fish, amphibians, birds, and other snakes; they usually swim with their head well out of the water.

Leatherback Sea Turtle, *Dermochelys coriacea*
Family Dermochelyidae (leatherback)
Size: Up to 90" long (carapace)
Range: Worldwide
Habitat: Pacific and Atlantic coasts and far-offshore waters

The only living species of its family, and the largest turtle on Earth, the Leatherback is an exceptionally large marine turtle with recorded weights of over 2,000 pounds. It is also extremely wide ranging, as its large size and physiological makeup allow it to tolerate both tropical and colder waters (in the United States it can be found as far north as Alaska and as far south as the Virgin Islands). Its "shell" is leathery or rubbery in texture, tapered in the rear; it is not divided into segments (scutes) but smooth, with five raised longitudinal ridges. It has an extended tail, and the limbs are clawless and flattened into large flippers. The color is mostly gray-brown to bluish black, with light spots or mottling, and pale on the underside. Juveniles have proportionately large limbs and are colored blackish with longitudinal white stripes down the back. Leatherbacks roam through primarily tropical but also subtropical seas, feeding mainly on jellyfish and other soft pelagic animals, at times diving over half a mile deep to find their prey. During the breeding season, females come ashore to lay up to 100 eggs in depressions that they dig into sandy beaches. This species is critically endangered because of nesting habitat destruction, entanglement in fishing nets casualties, and ingestion of trash.

Species Fun Fact!

Despite their wide range habitat, these turtles are currently endangered due to a number of reasons (many caused by humans).

Green Sea Turtle, *Chelonia mydas*
Family Cheloniidae (sea turtles)
Size: Up to 48" long (carapace)
Range: Worldwide
Habitat: Shallow to deep marine waters; Florida beaches to nest

Sometimes known as just the Green Turtle, this is a medium-size sea turtle with a broad, oval, smooth shell and elongated limbs flattened into powerful flippers. The upper shell (carapace) is brownish to olive green with variable, radiating striations; the lower shell (plastron) is pale tan to whitish. The common name refers to the greenish color of the turtle's fat. Green Turtles feed underwater for marine plants but must surface to breathe. The young hatch on their own and venture to the open ocean for a year before returning to coastal waters. These turtles are threatened partly because of destruction of nesting sites and entanglement in fishing nets.

Olive Ridley Sea Turtle, *Lepidochelys olivaceae*
Family Cheloniidae (sea turtles)
Size: Up to 26" long (carapace)
Range: Southern Atlantic and southern Pacific oceans
Habitat: Coastal and offshore tropical waters

Also known as the Pacific Ridley, the Olive Ridley is a relatively small sea turtle with a heart-shaped carapace with narrow lateral scutes and broad, flattened flippers with small claws. The tail is short in females but extends well beyond the carapace in males. They are grayish when young, but as adults they become deep olive green, with a paler plastron. Although highly migratory in the open ocean and solitary by nature, females come ashore in huge groups once a year to lay eggs at specific beach sites (none in the United States). They have powerful jaws to eat a variety of crustaceans, fish, and marine algae. Olive Ridleys are severely threatened by habitat destruction and entanglements in fishing nets.

Hawksbill Sea Turtle, *Eretmochelys imbricata*
Family Cheloniidae (sea turtles)
Size: Up to 36" long (carapace)
Range: Tropical Atlantic and Pacific Oceans
Habitat: Shallow offshore waters, especially near reefs; beaches to lay eggs

The Hawksbill is a small sea turtle with a distinctive, hooked snout that resembles the beak of a hawk. The carapace is roughly oval with a tapered rear end and is covered with ridged, pointed, overlapping scutes that are brown, golden, or greenish, with a mottled and radiating pattern. The plastron is pale yellow, and the limbs are flattened into long flippers with small claws. Hawksbills feed in relatively shallow waters, often in reefs, rocky areas, or lagoons, for sponges, other invertebrates, and algae, using their sharp beaks to pry into crevices. As with others in this family, females come ashore to lay eggs in a sandy pit. They are critically threatened, especially because of harvesting for "tortoiseshell" jewelry.

Loggerhead Sea Turtle, *Caretta caretta*
Family Cheloniidae (sea turtles)
Size: Up to 48" long (carapace)
Range: Southern California, Gulf of Mexico, most of Atlantic coast
Habitat: Warm coastal waters, estuaries; beaches to lay eggs

The Loggerhead is the largest of the hard-shelled turtles, capable of weighing up to 1000 pounds. The carapace is flattened, somewhat heart-shaped, with the broad end in front, and colored various shades of reddish to greenish brown. The head is large, the limbs are flattened into broad flippers, and the tail is long (extending well beyond the shell). An endangered species, Loggerheads are threatened by loss of sandy nesting habitat and by drownings in fishing nets. They eat a wide variety of food, including algae, sponges, jellyfish, crustaceans, and urchins, which they crush with their strong jaws.

Snapping Turtle, *Chelydra serpentina*
Family Chelydridae (snapping turtles)
Size: Up to 14" long (carapace)
Range: Most of United States east of the Rocky Mountains
Habitat: Most freshwater environments, especially with plentiful water plants

The Snapping Turtle is a large, stocky turtle with a relatively small shell for the body size; a long, tapered, heavily scaled tail; and a massive head with powerful jaws. The carapace color is variable but usually some shade of brown, often obscured by a coating of algae; the body parts are yellowish although the head is usually dark. The feet are strong, with long claws. Snapping Turtles may rest underwater on muddy bottoms or bask on rocks in the sun to warm themselves. During the winter they burrow into the muddy substrate of shallow ponds, although they are known to be active even in icy conditions. They forage for a wide variety of prey, including plants, insects, aquatic invertebrates, small mammals, amphibians, and birds. To ambush their prey, they sometimes bury themselves in the mud underwater leaving only their eyes and nostrils exposed, then snap up unsuspecting animals that comes close by. Use caution around this turtle, especially if it is taken out of water, as it can give a painful bite. The related Alligator Snapping Turtle has a heavily serrated carapace, as opposed to the relatively smooth carapace of the common Snapping Turtle. Many people relish the meat of this turtle in dishes and soups.

Species Fun Fact!

Snapping Turtles can grow up to 14 inches long, but, due to its large, stocky figure, its shell size is relatively small.

Alligator Snapping Turtle, *Macrochelys temminckii*
Family Chelydridae (snapping turtles)
Size: Up to 26" long (carapace)
Range: Central and southern United States
Habitat: Deep waters in rivers and ponds

The Alligator Snapping Turtle is among the world's largest freshwater turtles, with specimens reaching more than 200 pounds. It appears quite formidable, with a massive, nonretractile head; long, clawed limbs; and a long, rough tail. The relatively undersize carapace has three pronounced ridges with pointed scutes and is colored yellowish brown to gray, often with a cryptic coating of algae. The head has a pointed snout terminating in a sharp, hooked beak. Alligator Snapping Turtles spend almost their entire life in water, except when females come ashore to lay eggs. To feed, they remain motionless on the lake or river bottom with their mouth open, revealing a pink, worm-like appendage on the tongue that lures fish, frogs, and other turtles. They then quickly strike with their powerful jaws. This is a threatened species because of exploitation for meat and shells, as well as habitat destruction.

Florida Red-bellied Turtle, *Chrysemys nelsoni*

Family Emydidae (pond and box turtles)
Size: Up to 12" long (carapace)
Range: Florida and Georgia
Habitat: Stagnant fresh or brackish waters; ponds, swamps, mangroves

Found only in Florida and southern Georgia, the Florida Red-bellied Turtle is a large pond turtle with a thick, high-domed shell. The feet have webbed toes for swimming, with longer claws on the front feet, and the upper jaw has two, toothlike projections (only noticeable at close range). The upper shell (carapace) is blackish with rusty-red markings, the lower shell (plastron) is yellowish orange, and the body parts are black with yellow stripes. Florida Red-bellied Turtles spend much time basking on rocks or logs in the water and feed on aquatic plants.

Pond Slider, *Chrysemys scripta*
Family Emydidae (pond and box turtles)
Size: Up to 11" long (carapace)
Range: Southeastern United States; Texas to West Virginia
Habitat: Slow-moving stream and rivers, lakes and ponds with muddy bottoms

The Pond Slider is a common and gregarious pond turtle with a relatively flat carapace, webbed feet, and an unhinged plastron. Three distinct subspecies exist, all with greenish-yellow and dark green or black stripes or reticulations on the scutes and bright yellow, orange, or red markings behind the eyes. The familiar Red-eared Slider (illustrated) has a red, oval spot behind the eye. In older individuals, the colors become blackish and the markings diminish. Pond Sliders are active during the day, when they are fond of basking in groups on logs and rocks near water, sometimes stacked one atop the other, and "sliding" into water for safety if alarmed. Young turtles feed on a variety of small animals, insects, and aquatic invertebrates; adults favor plants. This is the turtle most popular in the pet trade and is now distributed in many areas outside its natural range.

Western Pond Turtle, *Actinemys marmorata*
Family Emydidae (pond and box turtles)
Size: Up to 8" long (carapace)
Range: Along the Pacific coast and inland; Washington to Mexico
Habitat: Ponds, lakes, and streams with muddy bottoms and plentiful aquatic vegetation

The Western Pond Turtle is a mostly aquatic pond turtle with a low, smooth, unkeeled carapace; an unhinged plastron; well-clawed feet; and a blunt head. The carapace is generally dark brown or olive, with thin, radiating yellowish marks or a marbled pattern; or it may lack the patterning and be plainly colored. The plastron is pale yellow; the legs and head are speckled in dark brown, black, and yellow. Males have a contrasting light throat, while the throat of females is dark. They aggressively defend prime basking sites but will leap to safely in the water at the slightest notice of an intruder. They are opportunistic feeders, eating most any available food, including aquatic plants, algae, insects, larvae, crayfish, and carrion.

Blandings Turtle, *Emydoidea blandingi*
Family Emydidae (pond and box turtles)
Size: Up to 10" long (carapace)
Range: Midwest and Great Lakes region
Habitat: Lakes, ponds, and streams with plentiful aquatic vegetation

The Blandings Turtle is a gentle pond turtle with an oblong, high-domed carapace that is slightly flat on top; a hinged plastron; a flat head with protruding, dark eyes; and a long neck. The carapace is dark grayish green to brownish, usually with many small yellow spots and dashes in a radiating pattern. The body is mostly dark, with a contrasting yellow chin, throat, and under-neck area. Males have a concave plastron and a longer tail than females. At home on land or in the water, Blandings Turtles often bask on shore, rocks, or stumps, quickly retreating to the safety of water if alarmed. They feed on all manner of insects, larvae, mollusks, and plants and spend the winter in the muddy bottoms of ponds, swamps, or streams. This is considered a threatened species because of loss of its wetland habitat.

Northern Map Turtle, *Graptemys geographica*
Family Emydidae (pond and box turtles)
Size: Up to 10" long (carapace)
Range: Midwestern United States
Habitat: Ponds, slow-moving streams and rivers, especially with abundant vegetation and muddy bottoms

The Northern Map Turtle is a medium-size pond turtle with a relatively smooth, broad carapace that is slightly ridged along the top (more so in juveniles). It is colored some shade of greenish brown or gray, with alternating light and dark thin concentric lines that resemble the contours of a topographic map, becoming less obvious with age. The head and limbs have yellowish stripes, and there is often a distinct yellow spot behind the eyes. The carapace of the male is shorter and narrower than that of the female. Northern Map Turtles are mostly active during the day and can be found basking on rocks or logs in small groups, even one on top of the other, but quickly disappear into the water when alarmed. They feed on insects and invertebrates, including snails and freshwater clams. In cold climates they become dormant during winter.

Painted Turtle, *Chrysemys picta*
Family Emydidae (pond and box turtles)
Size: Up to 10" long (carapace)
Range: Northern latitudes of western United States; most of eastern United States
Habitat: Ponds, lakes, marshes, slow-moving streams

The Painted Turtle is a widespread and common pond turtle found from coast to coast in the United States. The carapace is oval, flattened, non-keeled, and smooth and has a continuous (not serrated) rear margin. The rear legs are flattened with webbed toes; the front legs are stumpy with long claws (longer in males). The color of the carapace is olive-brown to blackish, with variable yellowish to reddish variegations and scute margins. The skin on the legs and head is dark green with yellow stripes, and the plastron is yellow to orange, with a broad black pattern in the center. Male Painted Turtles are considerably smaller than females. Highly aquatic and active during the day, they are often found basking on logs or rocks in groups, sometimes with turtles stacked one atop the other. At night they rest underwater, and in the winter they hibernate in the mud of shallow water. Females will often travel some distance from water to lay her eggs is a shallow depression, and the young are completely independent upon hatching. Adult Painted Turtles feed on plants and all manner of aquatic prey, including plants, invertebrates, and small amphibians—young turtles feed mostly on animal prey.

Species Fun Fact!

Painted Turtles truly are unique! Their shell coloring can differ from animal to animal, while the coloring on their skin is dark green with yellow stripes.

Spotted Turtle, *Clemmys guttata*
Family Emydidae (pond and box turtles)
Size: Up to 5" long (carapace)
Range: East-central United States; coastal plains to Florida
Habitat: Ponds, streams, marshes, meadows

The Spotted Turtle is a rather cute, small, semiaquatic pond turtle found on land or water, with an unkeeled, smooth, oval, flattened carapace. It is black, with very few or many scattered small yellow-orange dots. This spotting continues onto the head, limbs, and tail; the plastron is pale yellow heavily marked with black. Males have darker eyes and longer, thicker tails than females. Active during the day, Spotted Turtles feed mostly in the water for a wide variety of food, including plants, algae, invertebrates, and small fish or amphibians. They become dormant in cooler climates in winter, burrowing into underwater mud and debris, emerging in early spring when the water is still fairly cold.

Eastern Box Turtle, *Terrapene carolina*
Family Emydidae (pond and box turtles)
Size: Up to 6" long (carapace)
Range: Eastern United States except for the far northern latitudes
Habitat: Wet woodlands, fields, meadows, rural gardens

The Eastern Box Turtle has a terrestrial lifestyle, venturing into bogs or wetlands but not open water. It has a tall, domed carapace; a chunky, angular head; and short limbs and may have three or four toes on the hind feet. It is called a box turtle because the plastron has a lateral "hinge" that allows it to fold up tightly against the carapace, providing complete protection to the turtle's soft parts. The coloration is variable, having contrasting yellow, brown, and black markings in patterns that radiate from a corner of each scute and similar-colored spotting on the head and legs. Eastern Box Turtles feed on slugs, earthworms, plants, fruit, and even poisonous mushrooms, which can make their flesh deadly to eat.

Wood Turtle, *Glyptemys insulpta*
Family Emydidae (pond and box turtles)
Size: Up to 8" long (carapace)
Range: Great Lakes region to northeastern United States
Habitat: Shallow rivers and streams; associated fields and wetlands

At home on land and in the water, Wood Turtles range far north into Quebec and Nova Scotia. The carapace is brownish to gray with a slight ridge along the top, is rough in texture, and has individual scutes formed into raised, pyramid-shaped projections (overall appearing like an old piece of wood). The soft parts are grayish to black, with red coloring on the throat, underside of the neck, and at the base of the forelegs. The plastron is yellow with large black patches near the outer margin. Wood Turtles feed on plant matter, fruit, small animals, worms, and slugs, often roaming a considerable distance to forage. It is a threatened species because of collection for meat and habitat loss.

Diamondback Terrapin, *Malaclemys terrapin*
Family Emydidae (pond and box turtles)
Size: Up to 9" long (carapace)
Range: Coastal eastern United States; Texas to Connecticut
Habitat: Estuaries, salt marshes, lagoons

The Diamondback Terrapin is a strong-swimming pond turtle of coastal, brackish waters and the only member of this family in North America to tolerate salt water. The body is compact, with a thick head; bulging eyes; and enlarged, sturdy, flipper-like hind limbs. The carapace has prominent ridges along the back; deep, roughly diamond-shaped concentric grooves in each scute; and is colored plain gray-brown or black (sometimes with yellowish grooves). The plastron is unhinged and colored greenish yellow with blackish blotches. The head, limbs, and tail are pale gray, with variable black speckles or spots. Diamondback Terrapins rest in muddy bottoms during the night and emerge during the day, hunting for worms, crustaceans, mollusks, small fish, and plants. They have become threatened because of loss of their wetland habitat and consumption for meat.

Loggerhead Musk Turtle, *Sternotherus minor*
Family Kinosternidae (musk and mud turtles)
Size: Up to 5" long (carapace)
Range: Southeastern United States
Habitat: Ponds, rivers, swamps

The Loggerhead Musk Turtle (in some areas known as the Stripe-necked Musk Turtle) is a highly aquatic turtle of most freshwater habitats. It has a domed, slightly keeled carapace colored brownish gray or olive, with variable blackish spotting, radiating lines, or scute margins. The head is relatively large with small chin barbels, a long neck, and alternating dark gray and yellowish spots or stripes. Males have a long tail; that of the female is quite short. Loggerhead Musk Turtles spend most of their lives underwater, creeping along pond and creek bottoms and among vegetation, only occasionally basking at the surface. Broad jaws are used to crush mollusks, but the turtle will also eat a variety of invertebrates and plants. If provoked, musk turtles emit an odiferous secretion through glands under the outer edges of the carapace.

Smooth Softshell, *Apalone muticus*
Family Trionychidae (softshell turtles)
Size: Up to 14" long (carapace)
Range: Midwestern states to the Gulf Coast
Habitat: Rivers, large streams, lakes with sandy or muddy bottoms

Softshell turtles are known for the soft, leathery surface of the carapace in place of the hard, bony scutes found in typical turtles. The Smooth Softshell's carapace is nearly round and very flat, like a pancake. Its color is brownish to olive, with variable amounts of small darker spots and short marks. The head is small and rounded, with a pointed, tubular snout, and has a pale stripe behind the eye. The limbs are flattened like flippers for swimming and have three claws with webbing in between. Smooth Softshells are very fast swimmers and can remain submerged with only their snout above water to breathe, like a short snorkel. Wary by nature, they bask on sandy shores but quickly retreat to water if alarmed. They feed both in the water and on land for a wide variety of invertebrates, small fish, tadpoles, and plants.

Gopher Tortoise, *Gopherus polyphemus*
Family Testudinidae (tortoises)
Size: Up to 13" long (carapace)
Range: Far southeastern United States
Habitat: Sandy soils of open woodlands, scrubby grasslands, coastal dunes

The Gopher Tortoise is a terrestrial tortoise with a tall, domed upper shell (carapace) that has concentric ridges and grooves within the individual shell segments. The head is short-necked, rounded, and thick; the front legs are flattened, with heavy scales and claws, while the rear legs are short and stumpy. The carapace is brownish, the lower shell (plastron) is yellowish, and the body parts are gray-brown. Gopher Tortoises dig long burrows underground for shelter and in turn provide homes for many other animals, including burrowing owls, rodents, and snakes. They feed during the day for plants and, as a defense, can retract their head and legs completely into the shell.

AMPHIBIANS

Little Grass Frog, *Pseudacris ocularis*
Family Hylidae (tree frogs)
Size: Up to 0.75" long
Range: Florida and Atlantic coastal plains
Habitat: Grassy areas near ponds and swamps

North America's smallest frog, the Little Grass Frog is a good climber but restricted to areas of grasses and sedges. Its tiny, smooth-skinned body is variable shades of cryptically colored brown, green, or reddish, with a prominent dark stripe through the eyes and onto the sides of the body and often a darker stripe along the back that is joined to a triangular patch between the eyes. The belly is pale and unmarked. Excellent jumpers and active day or night, Little Grass Frogs forage among grasses and on the ground for a variety of insect prey. The voice is a very high-pitched, cricket-like tinkling sound that is inaudible to some people.

Pacific Tree Frog, *Psuedacris regilla*
Family Hylidae (tree frogs)
Size: Up to 2" long
Range: Pacific Northwest, California, Nevada
Habitat: Streamsides, lakes; fields, meadows, and woodlands near water

The Pacific Tree Frog is a medium-size tree frog, quite common in the far western United States, that is most at home creeping about vegetation near the ground. The toes are thin and end in circular tips with pads underneath to aid in clinging to plants; the back feet are slightly webbed. The skin is rough and can be colored green, brown, or nearly black, with variable amounts of darker blotches on the back, but there is always a black stripe through the eye and sometimes a dark triangular spot on top of the head. Males have a dark, extendible throat patch that inflates while singing. Interestingly, these frogs are capable of changing their color seasonally or within the course of hours. Hiding in leaves, logs, or rocks during the day, they are mostly active at night, hunting for insects and small invertebrates.

Barking Tree Frog, *Hyla gratiosa*
Family Hylidae (tree frogs)
Size: Up to 2.75" long
Range: Coastal plains of southeastern United States and the mid-Atlantic states; scattered inland sites
Habitat: Woodlands near marshy areas or ponds, lush wetlands

The Barking Tree Frog is relatively large for a tree frog and is well equipped for climbing, with sticky, disc-like pads on the toes. The body is quite plump, and the skin has a grainy quality. The color is usually dull to bright green but can also be shades of brown, gray, or tan, and there are usually many round dark spots. Individuals can also change their color quickly. A distinct whitish stripe runs from the upper jaw and across the lower body, below which is a grayish belly. Active at night, these frogs prefer to stay in treetops during warm summer months and spend the remainder of the season on the ground, in water, or in burrows, becoming dormant when temperatures are excessively hot, dry or cold. Breeding males call out a low-pitched honking or barking sound while they float on the surface of shallow water. At other times they will call from the treetops. They feed on a wide variety of insects that inhabit their watery or arboreal habitat. Barking Tree Frogs can be quite tame, and are indeed popular as terrarium pets.

Species Fun Fact!

Barking Tree Frogs find their voices at night. Breeding males "bark" (some call it a low-pitched honking sound) from treetops or the surface of water.

Spring Peeper, *Pseudacris crucifer*
Family Hylidae (tree frogs)
Size: Up to 1.5" long
Range: Throughout eastern United States; Canada to the Gulf of Mexico
Habitat: Woodlands and grassy areas near ponds or swamps

The Spring Peeper is a small, common tree frog of eastern North America, capable of climbing but mostly found on the ground or in low vegetation. It has some webbing on the feet and enlarged discs on the toes to aid in gripping. The color can be reddish brown, dark brown, grayish, or olive, with faint dark marks on the upperside and legs and a distinctive, dark X pattern across the back. Depending on the region, the belly can be plain or spotted. Spring Peepers are active at night, with males perched near the water calling in spring with their familiar high-pitched peeping jingling chorus. They hunt for a variety of insects and spiders.

Northern Cricket Frog, *Acris crepitans*
Family Hylidae (tree frogs)
Size: Up to 1.5" long
Range: Most of eastern and central United States
Habitat: Warm, shallow streams and ponds

The Northern Cricket Frog is a small, ground-dwelling member of the tree frog family with bumpy, rough skin and partially webbed rear feet. Its color varies considerably, being some combination of mottled and patchy browns, greens, black, and reds, with a paler belly. There is often a distinct triangular mark between the eyes and a whitish stripe below the eyes that extends to the front legs. This frog is not a climber, but it is an excellent jumper (can leap up to 3 feet) and swimmer. Active during the day in water and on the ground, it sometimes basks in groups along shores and feeds on small insects and aquatic invertebrates. Its voice is a steely, clicking sound, presumably resembling that of a cricket.

Chorus Frog, *Pseudacris triseriata*
Family Hylidae (tree frogs)
Size: Up to 1.5" long
Range: Most of the United States east of the Rocky Mountains, into central Canada
Habitat: Grassy areas near water, meadows, marshes, lakes

The Chorus Frog is a small member of the tree frog family, although it is largely a ground dweller. Its tiny size and cryptic coloration make it difficult to spot, but its distinctive call can be heard from far away. The body is plump, with a relatively large head, thin legs, and unwebbed toes. The skin is smooth, olive to brown above, pale below, and typically with three broad, darker stripes along the back, which may be broken or nearly absent in some populations. On the head is a dark stripe through the eye and a whitish line above the jaw. The underside is whitish, sometimes with darker spotting, and males have a pale yellowish throat patch that appears dark when not inflated. Active in evenings and through the night, the common name is derived from the short, trilled calls that are often sung in the company of others (as in a chorus). The sound they make is often likened to running a finger along the length of a fine comb. The Chorus Frogs lurk among vegetation, around water, and under logs and rocks, hunting for small prey such as insects, worms, and spiders. During cold months and to hide, they can be found in burrows, under rocks and logs, or buried in leaf litter. If alarmed, they will quickly stop their chorus and head for the safety of water.

Species Fun Fact!

These critters truly do sing in unison! Their short, trilled calls are often sung with others in the area, sending off choir-like sounds.

Bullfrog, *Rana catesbeiana*
Family Ranidae (true frogs)
Size: Up to 6" long
Range: Throughout the central and eastern United States; also along the West Coast and in the Southwest
Habitat: Ponds and lakes with dense vegetation

The Bullfrog is North America's largest frog, endemic to virtually the entire expanse of the eastern United States and introduced to regions in the west, where it readily adapts to areas of human habitation. They are, however, always found near a body of water. It is squat and heavy bodied, with massive rear legs with webbed feet that allow quick and strong leaps and quick swimming. Its smooth skin is green to brownish green, with brown or gray mottling or spotting and a pale belly. It has large external eardrums just behind the eyes; in males, these are larger than the eyes, but in females they are of equal size or smaller than the eyes. Bullfrogs are mostly nocturnal and prefer warmer weather; during cold periods they will construct a small burrow in the mud and hibernate. They wait motionless for prey to come near, when their large mouths and long tongues enable them to feed on a wide variety of prey, including insects, aquatic invertebrates, and even small mammals, birds, or other bullfrogs. Their adaptability to new habitats and prolific breeding behavior has created problems in some areas, where they outcompete native frogs for resources.

Species Fun Fact!

Gross alert! In addition to feeding on other prey—the usual stuff like insects, small mammals, etc.— bullfrogs have been known to feed on . . . other bullfrogs!

Southern Leopard Frog, *Lithobates sphenocephalus*
Family Ranidae (true frogs)
Size: Up to 4" long
Range: South-central United States and East Coast to New York
Habitat: Freshwater or brackish marshes, streams, ponds, moist fields

The Southern Leopard Frog is a squat, boney frog with narrow hindquarters and long, powerful rear legs for leaping. There are two pale narrow ridges of skin along either side of the back and a light stripe above the mouth; the eardrums usually have a light-colored central spot. The overall color of its smooth skin is green to brownish, with large dark spots bordered by a lighter color, giving the frog its common name. Leopard Frogs skulk in the water or vegetation foraging for insects and invertebrates. Their large mouths allow them to eat fairly large prey, including small birds and other frogs.

Pickerel Frog, *Rana palustris*
Family Ranidae (true frogs)
Size: Up to 4" long
Range: Throughout the eastern United States except Florida
Habitat: Ponds, lakes, slow-moving streams, lush wetlands, grasslands near water

The Pickerel Frog is closely related to the Leopard Frog, with smooth skin and long, powerful hind legs. It is greenish brown to tan, with dark brown bars and spots overall, distinct pale dorsolateral folds, and two rows of square dark spots along the back (as opposed to the circular spots in the Leopard Frog). The belly is whitish, there is a bright yellow-orange wash where the inner thigh meets the body, and a pale stripe defines the upper jaw. Pickerel Frogs spend most of their lives on land, foraging for insects, spiders, sowbugs, and aquatic invertebrates. The call of the males sounds somewhat like a low-pitched snore. This frog secretes a poisonous chemical from its skin, which is capable of irritating the skin and is a useful deterrent against predators.

Wood Frog, *Rana sylvatica*
Family Ranidae (true frogs)
Size: Up to 3" long
Range: Throughout northern North America and Alaska; south to the Appalachian Mountains
Habitat: Depends on region; woodlands, grassy areas, tundra

The Wood Frog is a widespread frog of northerly latitudes, ranging as far north as the Arctic Circle—the only North American frog to do so. The skin is brown to greenish overall, with darker spots and mottling, sometimes with a pale stripe down the back. The dorso-lateral folds are distinct, and the belly is pale. Most striking is a black mask across the eyes, which extends to the eardrum, and a pale stripe on the upper jaw. Adapted to a mainly terrestrial existence, the rear toes are not fully webbed. Quite active and excellent jumpers, they feed on a wide variety of insects, other invertebrates, and plant matter. To survive in cold climates, Wood Frogs have exquisite physiology that allows most of their body tissue to freeze during winter hibernation and then thaw as spring arrives.

Columbia Spotted Frog, *Rana luteiventris*
Family Ranidae (true frogs)
Size: Up to 4" long
Range: Northwestern United States; south to Nevada and Utah
Habitat: Ponds, streams, lakes, and surrounding habitats

The Columbia Spotted Frog is a medium-size frog that is always found close to a permanent water source. It has relatively short legs, webbed hind toes, eyes that turn slightly upwards on the head, and well-developed dorsolateral folds along either side of the back. The skin color ranges from tan, brown, olive green, or reddish, depending on age and environment, and has small dark spots with lighter raised centers. The underside is pale pinkish or orangey, and the upper part of the jaw is whitish. Active day and night, this frog lurks in water or nearby vegetation in search of insects and other invertebrates. A slow-moving frog, it relies more on stealth and secrecy than quickness to avoid predation.

Pig Frog, *Rana grylio*
Family Ranidae (true frogs)
Size: Up to 6" long
Range: Coastal plains of the southeastern United States
Habitat: Ponds, marshes, swamps, lakesides with dense vegetation

The Pig Frog is a relative of the bullfrogs with a distinctive low, grunting call that resembles the sound of a pig. The body is large, with powerful hind legs, fully webbed hind toes, and a pointy snout. The eardrum on males is much larger that the eye, while on females it is about the size of the eye. Dorsolateral folds are not present. The skin is smooth, olive green to brownish, with variable amounts of darker mottling overall and a pale belly. Across the inner thigh is a pale stripe or a strip of pale spots. The similar Bullfrog usually shows spotting on the inner thigh but no distinct stripe. Active during the night, Pig Frogs are mostly aquatic but also quite comfortable on land and feed on a wide variety of insects, fish, amphibians, and aquatic invertebrates, especially crayfish. Prolific breeders, females can lay as many as 10,000 eggs in a mass on aquatic plants. Pig Frogs are commonly hunted in the South for their legs.

Species Fun Fact!

No, that's not the sound of a pig that you're hearing! That low, grunting call is actually the sound of the Pig Frog, which can lay as many as 10,000 eggs in one sitting.

Eastern Narrow-mouthed Frog, *Gastrophryne carolinensis*
Family Microhylidae (narrow-mouthed frogs)
Size: Up to 1.5" long
Range: Southeastern United States; Texas to Maryland
Habitat: A variety of moist areas near a water source

The Eastern Narrow-mouthed Frog is a small, secretive frog with a plump body; smooth skin; a narrow, tapered head; small eyes; and short, strong hind limbs for digging. There is also a curious small fold of skin across the top of the head, a characteristic of the group that can move forward to protect the eyes from biting ants. The color is highly variable and can change depending on environment and mood of the frog, but it is generally mottled grayish to reddish brown to black, with a speckled belly. Often two broad lighter patches are seen across each upper side. Males have a dark throat, whereas females have a light throat. These frogs hide during the day under rocks and logs or in burrows, becoming active at night in search of ants, their favored food. They quickly burrow into soil or decaying vegetation on the ground if alarmed.

Southern Toad, *Anaxyrus terrestris*
Family Bufonidae (toads)
Size: Up to 3.5" long
Range: Throughout coastal plains of the southeastern United States
Habitat: Sandy pine-oak woodlands, marshes, rural gardens

The Southern Toad is a medium-size, stocky toad with conspicuous protuberances behind the eyes and enlarged, oval raised lumps (parotoid glands) behind the eardrums. The skin is dry; covered with warts; and variably brown, gray, or nearly black, with dark spotting and a paler belly (males have a dark throat). Often there is a thin pale dorsal stripe running the length of the back. Southern Toads keep to burrows during the day, emerging at night to feed on insects and other invertebrates. They have an alarming high-pitched, trilled voice.

Great Plains Toad, *Anaxyrus cognatus*
Family Bufonidae (toads)
Size: Up to 4.5" long
Range: Central plains states from Wyoming to Mexico; west to California
Habitat: Prairies, desert scrub, farmlands, areas with loose soils and ephemeral water sources

The Great Plains Toad is a large, plump burrowing toad that may spend much of its life underground, especially during dry weather. The two raised cranial crests atop the head converge in front to form a knob on the upper snout, while in back they diverge to the parotoid glands. The skin is rough; covered with small warts; and colored pale brown, gray, or olive, with symmetrically arranged darker blotches with light borders across the back. The belly is unmarked white. Active at night, Great Plains Toads eat earthworms and insects, especially the destructive cutworm that can devastate crops. In breeding season during summer rains, males vocalize their long, drawn-out, high-pitched trilling song.

American Toad, *Bufo americanus*
Family Bufonidae (toads)
Size: Up to 4" long
Range: Eastern United States except for the far South
Habitat: Most moist habitats; woodlands, grassy areas, gardens near a water source

The American Toad is a common toad found throughout residential gardens in the East. The body is plump and squat, with rough, warty skin and two prominent parotoid glands above and behind the eardrums. The cranial crests between the eyes are not in contact with the parotoid glands and lack the knobs that are present in the similar Southern Toad. The color varies, being some combination of brown, reddish, or olive, with both dark and light spots and mottling and sometimes with a lighter stripe down the back. The belly is spotted. American Toads breed in spring, when males call out with a trilled, cricket-like song. They are most active at night, hiding in vegetation, rocks, or burrows during the day, feasting on insects, spiders, and worms.

Green Toad, *Bufo debilis*
Family Bufonidae (toads)
Size: Up to 2" long
Range: Most of Texas; north to Kansas and west to southeastern Arizona
Habitat: Arid prairies, rocky areas, foothills

The Green Toad is a small, secretive burrowing toad of dry habitats, using ephemeral pools and streams to breed. The body is somewhat flattened, with rough, warty skin colored bright green or yellow-green with small black spots and a white belly. The black spots do not coalesce to broad reticulations as in the similar Sonoran Green Toad. The parotoid glands are large, extending well down the sides of the body; cranial crests are absent. The throat of males is dark, whereas in females it is whitish. Active at night or in twilight hours, these frogs keep to the shelter of burrows or rocks during the heat of day and feed on a variety of insects and other invertebrates. The call is a buzzy, cricket-like trill.

Western Spadefoot Toad, *Spea hammondi*
Family Pelobatidae (spadefoot toads)
Size: Up to 2.5" long
Range: New Mexico, into Arizona and Texas; also western California
Habitat: Dry, grassy plains; sandy or gravelly areas

The spadefoots are so called because they possess a small, hard, spade-like projection on the bottom of each hind foot, which is used to help excavate burrows. The Western Spadefoot has a squat body with large, protruding eyes with vertical pupils; smoother skin than the true toads; and no parotoid glands. The color is gray, brown, or greenish, with variable darker blotches and spots that sometimes form indistinct lines down the back. The spots often contain orange-tipped warts; the belly is unmarked white. Spadefoots remain in burrows during the day and in times of dry weather, emerging at night and during periods of rain to feed on a variety of insects and worms. They have a quick breeding schedule, suitable for producing young in temporary, seasonal pools. The skin of these toads secretes a chemical that can cause allergy-like symptoms in humans.

Long-toed Salamander, *Ambystoma macrodactylum*
Family Ambystomatidae (mole salamanders)
Size: Up to 6.5" long
Range: Pacific Northwest; also in an isolated region near Santa Cruz, California
Habitat: Quite varied; coniferous forests, meadows, dry sagebrush near streams or ponds

The Long-toed Salamander is a small, adaptable mole salamander found from sea level to rocky, high-mountain regions. The body has smooth, shiny skin; a thick base to the head; a slightly flattened tail; and noticeably long, thin toes. The color is black on the back, speckled with white on the sides, and grayish below. Depending on the subspecies, there is a green, yellow, or light brown stripe down the middle of the back that is continuous or broken into spots. Usually active year-round but quite secretive, these salamanders live under rocks, leaf litter, and rotting wood and in burrows; they feed on worms, insects, small fish, and other amphibians. They coil up and twitch their tails when provoked and may detach their tail to distract predators. Otherwise fairly abundant, the Santa Cruz population is critically threatened.

Tiger Salamander, *Ambystoma tigrinum*
Family Ambystomatidae (mole salamanders)
Size: Up to 13" long
Range: Throughout most of the United States except for the far West and northeastern states
Habitat: Quite varied; forests, grasslands, sageland, wetlands

The Tiger Salamander is the largest land-dwelling salamander in the world, with a wide variation in color and pattern. The body is robust and rounded, with a broad, blunt head; small eyes; smooth, shiny skin; and a long tail (longer in males). There are six recognized subspecies, each with markedly different appearance, ranging from black or brown with yellowish cross bars or whitish spots, pale brown with black barring, or pea green with black blotches. Tiger Salamanders spend most of their lives in deep burrows made by rodents, emerging during late-winter rains and migrating to pools or streams to breed. They feed on insects, worms, other amphibians, and small rodents.

Spotted Salamander, *Ambystoma maculatum*
Family Ambystomatidae (mole salamanders)
Size: Up to 9.5" long
Range: Throughout the eastern United States except Florida
Habitat: Moist, deciduous woodlands

The Spotted Salamander is a very large, secretive salamander that remains underground for much of its life, and not frequently seen. The body is robust, with a long, thick tail; blunt head; small limbs; and many costal grooves along the abdomen. The smooth, moist skin is black, brown, or dark gray, with a paler underside and two rows of large circular yellow-orange spots along the sides. These salamanders remain in burrows made by other animals (they are not proficient diggers themselves) or among rocks, leaf litter and logs for most of the year, emerging when early spring rains provide pools in which to breed and raise young. They may travel more than 100 yards for this purpose, and only lay their eggs in these temporary pools to avoid the possibility of fish feeding on the eggs, although they are still susceptible to attack by wading birds, snakes, and other salamanders. The larvae are fully aquatic, having gills, tiny legs, and flattened tails, and undergo metamorphosis before reaching their terrestrial state. They hunt during the night on a diet of earthworms and insects, aided by their keen sense of smell and a sticky tongue to help grasp their prey. If provoked, they will secrete a mildly toxic, whitish fluid from glands in the back and tail that deters predators. Like many salamanders, they are very sensitive to increased acidity in their environment, and are also threatened by habitat loss and hunters for the pet trade.

Species Fun Fact!

These secretive salamanders, who hide for much of their lives, are hunted for humans in the pet trade.

Pacific Giant Salamander, *Dicamptodon ensatus*
Family Dicamptodontidae (giant salamanders)
Size: Up to 12" long
Range: Pacific coast region from central California to Canada; also around northern Idaho
Habitat: Streams, lakes, and springs in cool, moist woodlands

Although smaller than the Tiger Salamander, and previously placed in the same family, the Pacific Giant Salamander is still a very large, imposing salamander. The body is thick, with a long, flattened tail; oversize, blunt head; and indistinct costal grooves. The smooth, moist skin is brown (sometimes with a violet cast) above, pale brown or creamy below, with variable dark mottling and blotches that sometimes form a netlike pattern on the back and sides. Active day or night and comfortable in water or on land, these salamanders hide under vegetation, rocks, and rotting logs feeding on insects, other amphibians, snakes, and even small mammals. Although most salamanders are incapable of vocalization, this species can emit a low yelping sound when provoked.

California Slender Salamander, *Batrachoseps attenuatus*
Family Plethodontidae (lungless salamanders)
Size: Up to 5.5" long
Range: California coastal foothills into southern Oregon; also Sierra Nevada
Habitat: Moist woodlands and fields, especially near redwoods

The California Slender Salamander is a small, very thin salamander with a long, rounded tail; small head and eyes; and tiny, thin limbs. As with the other lungless salamanders, it absorbs oxygen through its moist, slimy skin and has distinct costal grooves along the length of its body. The color is gray-brown to black overall, with a paler wide dorsal stripe that varies from brown, reddish, to yellowish, and is often marked with thin, darker, forward-pointing chevrons. The belly is dark with fine white specks; the underside of the tail is creamy white. Especially active during periods of rain, slender salamanders lurk among leaf litter and moist logs or roots to hunt for earthworms, spiders, and other invertebrates. They are often found motionless in a tight coil and then quickly and erratically squirm away, even detaching their tail to distract predators.

Red Salamander, *Pseudotriton ruber*
Family Plethodontidae (lungless salamanders)
Size: Up to 7" long
Range: Eastern United States; Pennsylvania to Alabama
Habitat: Woodlands with streams, ponds, wetlands

The Red Salamander is a stout, thick-bodied salamander with a relatively short tail and short limbs. The color varies depending on age, being bright orange-red when young and gradually darkening to brownish purple in maturity. In all stages, the body is covered in small, irregular black spots, and the eyes are light yellow. A lungless salamander, it has smooth, shiny skin and distinct costal grooves. Mostly terrestrial, it lives under leaf litter and rocks except during breeding season, when it migrates to aquatic habitats. It feeds on earthworms, insects, and even other salamanders. Red Salamanders assume a defensive posture when provoked, raising their tails and curling back their heads; the skin secretes a toxic fluid.

Slimy Salamander, *Plethodon glutinosus*
Family Plethodontidae (lungless salamanders)
Size: Up to 8" long
Range: Throughout most of the eastern United States
Habitat: Shaded woodlands, streamsides, rocky ravines

Aptly named, the Slimy Salamander has skin that is coated with a slimy, glue-like secretion that is thought to be protective as well as a deterrent to predators. The body shape is similar to that of other lungless salamanders—medium-size, with relatively short limbs and evident costal grooves. The color is shiny black with irregular small white or yellowish spots on the sides, back, head, and tail. The underside is grayish. Active at night, or during the day after rains, Slimy Salamanders generally stay under rocks and logs or in burrows made by other animals. Secretive and territorial, they feed on a variety of invertebrates and insects, especially ants.

Cave Salamander, *Eurycea lucifuga*
Family Plethodontidae (lungless salamanders)
Size: Up to 7" long
Range: East-central United States
Habitat: Areas with limestone caves and surrounding woodlands

The Cave Salamander is a thin, climbing salamander with a long, rounded, grasping tail; blunt head; and long limbs. It has the typical smooth, shiny skin and costal grooves of the lungless salamander family. Quite striking in color, the skin is dull yellow-brown to bright reddish orange, with a paler belly and dark spots on the back and sides, which sometimes merge into stripes on either side. Juveniles are paler overall, and the color becomes more saturated as they mature. Although favoring the walls and ledges of the dimly lit parts of limestone caves (known as the "twilight zone"), Cave Salamanders will venture into surrounding areas, seeking protection under rocks or rotting wood. Eggs are laid in pools or springs inside of caves, and the hatchlings are fully aquatic, with gills and finlike tails, until they metamorphose into the adult, terrestrial form. They eat worms, insects, crustaceans, and other invertebrates, which they capture by lunging and a quick flick of the tongue. When disturbed, they will coil up their body and wag a raised tail, sometimes even detaching their tail, which will soon regenerate. This species is endangered or threatened in some states, mostly due to habitat loss or contamination of water. It has an alternate name of the Spotted-tail Salamander, and should not be confused with other species of cave-dwelling salamander, which are sometimes referred to as simply "cave salamander" (another good case for scientific names).

Species Fun Fact!

These little critters become more beautiful as they age—juveniles start out paler than their adult counterparts, but the color becomes more saturated as they mature.

Dusky Salamander, *Desmognathus fuscus*
Family Plethodontidae (lungless salamanders)
Size: Up to 5.5" long
Range: New England south to Louisiana, excluding southeastern coastal plains
Habitat: Moist woodlands near streams or springs

The Dusky Salamander is a medium-size, stout salamander with strong front limbs and a relatively short, triangular, flattened tail. As a lungless salamander, it also has the typical smooth, shiny skin and evident costal grooves. The color ranges from light brown, reddish brown, to dark brown, with variable amounts of blackish spots and mottling, which sometimes merge to form stripes on the sides. Generally, a vague light stripe can be seen from the back of the eye to the base of the mouth. Dusky Salamanders keep to the cover of logs and rocks during the day, emerging at night to forage for worms and insects near water. They are active year round except in colder climates, where they burrow to escape freezing weather. Capable of moving quickly and jumping well to avoid predation, these salamanders will also detach their tail to distract predators.

Arboreal Salamander, *Aneides lugubris*
Family Plethodontidae (lungless salamanders)
Size: Up to 7" long
Range: Coastal region and Sierra Nevada of California
Habitat: Oak and pine woodlands, sand dunes, marshes

Called the Arboreal Salamander for good reason, this species is an excellent climber, with expanded, squarish toes and a round, curling, grasping tail. As with others in this family, it lack lungs, absorbing oxygen through the skin, and has a small groove between the nostril and the upper lip. The head is large compared to the body, and the jaw is laden with sharp teeth that can cause a painful bite. The color is brown above, with small, pale yellow dots; the underside is whitish, gray, or creamy. Arboreal Salamanders stay in the moist nooks in trees or in leaf litter, venturing out when the weather is wet to feed on insects, worms, snails, and occasionally other salamanders, which they snatch with their tongues.

Green Salamander, *Aneides aeneus*
Family Plethodontidae (lungless salamanders)
Size: Up to 5" long
Range: Appalachian Mountain region of the eastern United States
Habitat: Sandstone rock outcroppings and cliffs

The Green Salamander is a medium-size salamander with a slightly flattened body, thick head, large eyes, and squarish toe tips for traction on steep rock faces. It is a member of the lungless salamander family, all of which lack lungs and absorb oxygen through their thin, slippery skin. The color mimics the color of lichens and moss where these salamanders live, with bright yellow-green mottling over a black background. The underside is pale gray to creamy and mostly unmarked. Green Salamanders keep protected in rocks and crevices or under wood during the day, becoming active at night, deftly moving along vertical rock cliffs and up trees, searching for insects, snail, and slugs. They spend the winter in hibernation.

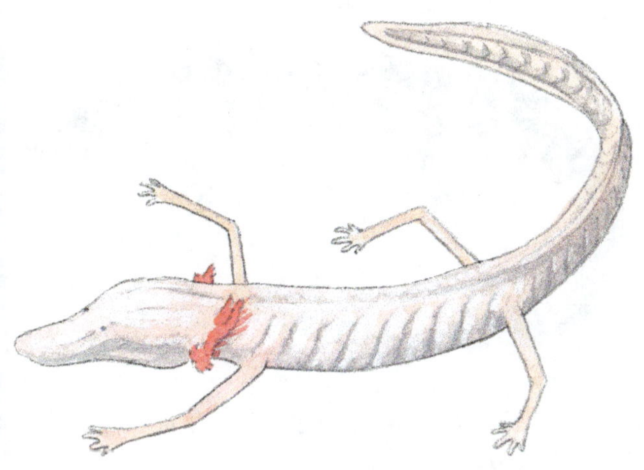

Texas Blind Salamander, *Typhlomolge rathbuni*
Family Plethodontidae (lungless salamanders)
Size: Up to 5" long
Range: A single region in central Texas
Habitat: Underground stream systems in caves

The Texas Blind Salamander is a bizarre-looking amphibian that spends its life underwater in complete darkness and is found only in a single cave network of the Edwards Aquifer in Texas. It remains in its larval stage throughout its life, retaining gills to breathe underwater and having only vestigial, sightless eyes represented by black dots under the skin. The body is thin, with a pointed snout; flattened head; fin-like tail; and long, dainty legs. It is colored translucent whitish to pale pink overall, with bright red gills. It feeds on aquatic invertebrates and plankton that are nourished by the guano of bats that cohabit their caves. It is considered an endangered species because of the vulnerability of its extremely limited range.

Eastern Newt, *Notophthalmus viridescens*
Family Salamandridae (newts)
Size: Up to 3.5" long
Range: Throughout the eastern United States
Habitat: Wetlands, ponds, nearby meadows or woodlands

Newts are elongate, short-legged, long-tailed, semiaquatic relatives of the salamanders with dry, rough-textured skin, except in their aquatic phases. They are born in the water, mature on land, and then return to the water at adulthood. The Eastern Newt comprises several subspecies and has a coloration that varies from orange in the immature stage to greenish brown to blackish in the adult, with a dark orange belly and numerous tiny black spots overall. Newts are adept swimmers, propelled by undulating their bodies and their long, flattened tails. They forage day or night in the water or on the ground for insects, larvae, fish or frog eggs, and worms. They may burrow or remain active in the water during winter.

California Newt, *Taricha torosa*
Family Salamandridae (newts)
Size: Up to 7.5" long
Range: California coast and coastal foothills; Sierra Nevada
Habitat: Woodlands of oak, redwood, and pine near streams or ponds

The California Newt is typical of the newts with its generally dry, rough skin and lack of distinct costal grooves. It has a stocky body and is colored light brown to reddish brown above and yellow-orange below, with little contrast in between. The lower eyelids and eyes are pale. During breeding season, males develop smooth skin; a flattened tail; dark, rough patches on the inner thigh; and an enlarged vent (anal area). California Newts lurk in leaf litter and burrows made by other animals, roaming farther during rainy weather, and come to a water source to breed. When alarmed, they present a defensive posture, raising their front end and tail to reveal the brightly colored belly and throat. They feed on earthworms, insects, and amphibian eggs.

Red-bellied Newt, *Taricha rivularis*
Family Salamandridae (newts)
Size: Up to 7.5" long, including tail
Range: Northern California coast and inland foothills
Habitat: Redwood forest near streams

The Red-bellied Newt is a stout, large-limbed salamander that is similar in appearance to the California Newt. It has rough, dry skin that is dark brown to black above, deep red below, with a dark band running under the vent (anal area). The eyes are mostly dark, compared to the lighter eyes of the California Newt. Males in breeding season have smoother skin; flattened tails; rough, dark patches at the inner thigh; and pads under the toes. These newts are largely terrestrial except during breeding season, when they frequent water; they mostly keep to underground burrows. If provoked, Red-bellied Newts demonstrate a defensive posture of curling back and raising the front end of their body, exposing the bright, colorful underside. The skin contains a powerful toxin that deters predators.

Mudpuppy, *Necturus maculosus*
Family Proteidae (mudpuppies and waterdogs)
Size: Up to 17" long
Range: Most of the eastern United States, except coastal states
Habitat: Bottoms of ponds and streams with plentiful aquatic vegetation

The Mudpuppy is a common, entirely aquatic salamander with bushy, deep red gills that maintains a larval condition through-out its life. The body is fairly large, with a flat head; small limbs; and a short, laterally compressed tail. The color is brown to black-ish above, whitish below, and covered with variable amounts of blackish spots and mottling. Mudpuppies stay hidden during the day among underwater plants, logs, and rocks, venturing out at night and crawling along bottoms or swimming like a fish. They feed on all manner of aquatic prey, including worms, snails, cray-fish, small fish, and other amphibians. They are also known as waterdogs because some think their squeaky vocalization sounds like a barking dog.

Greater Siren, *Siren lacertina*
Family Sirenidae (sirens)
Size: Up to 38" long
Range: Southeastern coastal plains from Virginia to Alabama
Habitat: Murky, weedy ponds, streams, and swamps

The sirens are entirely aquatic, thick-bodied, tubular, eel-like amphibians with one pair of diminutive front limbs, gill slits, and gills for breathing underwater. The tail is flattened and ridged with thin fins. There are also conspicuous costal grooves, a rounded head, and small eyes. The Greater Siren is quite large, gray or greenish overall, darkest along the back, with variable amounts of small yellowish and black spots and mottling. It stays hidden in submerged weeds and muddy bottoms, venturing out at night to feed on small animals, invertebrates, and aquatic detritus. If its habitat dries up, it will secrete a protective coating and burrow into the mud until water returns.

Reptiles and Amphibians by Region

Throughout the United States

Bullfrog
Common Garter Snake
Common Kingsnake
Gopher Snake
Painted Turtle
Racer
Ringneck Snake
Tiger Salamander
Wood Frog

Eastern United States

American Toad
Chorus Frog
Copperhead
Diamondback Terrapin
Dusky Salamander
Eastern Box Turtle
Eastern Fence Lizard
Eastern Hognose Snake
Eastern Newt
Five-lined Skink
Green Salamander
Milk Snake
Mudpuppy
Northern Cricket Frog
Northern Water Snake
Pickerel Frog
Queen Snake
Red Salamander
Six-lined Racerunner
Slimy Salamander
Snapping Turtle
Southern Leopard Frog
Spotted Salamander
Spotted Turtle
Spring Peeper

Western United States

Arboreal Salamander
California Newt
California Slender Salamander
Great Plains Toad
Pacific Giant Salamander
Red-bellied Newt
Side-blotched Lizard
Striped Whipsnake
Western Pond Turtle
Western Rattlesnake
Western Skink
Western Whiptail

Central United States

Alligator Snapping Turtle
Blandings Turtle
Cave Salamander
Corn Snake
Northern Map Turtle
Smooth Softshell
Texas Horned Lizard
Wood Turtle

Southwestern United States

Chuckwalla
Collared Lizard
Cottonmouth
Desert Night Lizard
Gila Monster
Greater Earless Lizard
Long-nosed Leopard Lizard
Long-nosed Snake
Rosy Boa
Sidewinder
Texas Blind Salamander
Western Banded Gecko
Western Blind Snake
Western Shovel-nosed Snake

Southeastern United States

American Alligator
American Crocodile
Barking Tree Frog
Eastern Coral Snake
Eastern Narrow-mouthed Frog
Florida Red-bellied Turtle
Gopher Tortoise
Greater Siren
Green Anole
Green Toad
Little Grass Frog
Loggerhead Musk Turtle
Mediterranean House Gecko
Mole Skink
Pig Frog
Pond Slider
Rough Green Snake
Scarlet Snake
Southern Toad
Western Slender Glass Lizard
Western Spadefoot

Northwestern United States

Columbia Spotted Frog
Long-toed Salamander
Northern Alligator Lizard
Pacific Tree Frog
Rubber Boa

Oceans

Green Sea Turtle
Hawksbill Sea Turtle
Leatherback Sea Turtle
Loggerhead Sea Turtle
Olive Ridley Sea Turtle

Index

About the Author/Illustrator

Todd Telander is a naturalist/illustrator/ artist living in Walla Walla, Washington. He has studied and illustrated wildlife since 1989 while living in California, Colorado, New Mexico, and Washington. He graduated from the University of California, Santa Cruz, with degrees in biology, environmental studies, and scientific illustration and has since illustrated numerous books and other publications, including FalconGuides'  Scats and Tracks series. His wife, Kirsten Telander, is a writer; they have two sons, Miles and Oliver. His work can be viewed online at toddtelander.com or telandergallery.com.